MW01382660

BLUE GHOST MEMOIRS

USS LEXINGTON CV-16

1943 - 1945

Otto C. Romanelli
Lt. Cdr. USNR Ret.

Turner Publishing Company
Publishers of America's History
P.O. Box 3101
Paducah, Kentucky 42002-3101

Co-published by
Mark A. Thompson, Associate Publisher

For book publishing write to:
M.T. Publishing Company, Inc.
P.O. Box 6802
Evansville, Indiana 47719-6802

Author: Otto C. Romanelli
Pre-Press work by M.T. Publishing Company, Inc.
Graphic Designer: Amanda J. Eads

Copyright © 2002
Turner Publishing Company

This book or any part thereof may not be reproduced without the written consent of the author and the publishers.

The materials were compiled and produced using available information; Turner Publishing Company, M.T. Publishing Company, Inc., and Otto C. Romanelli regret they cannot assume liability for errors or omissions.

Library of Congress
Control Number: 2002116010

ISBN: 1-56311-848-3

Printed in the United States of America

Limited Edition

Table of Contents

Illustrations

DEDICATION

*To all the men and women, who
"Go down to the sea in ships"
to serve their country in the
cause of liberty ... and especially to
those who lie in watery graves.*

ACKNOWLEDGMENTS

I want to acknowledge my appreciation to Captain Edward Steichen, USNR (Ret.) for the fine photographs he and his assistant took during their brief visit aboard the USS *Lexington,* some of which I have taken the liberty of reproducing in this volume. Little could I have appreciated at the time, the beauty of those photographs as I escorted him around the Gunnery Department equipment.

I have a deep sense of obligation to three other retired Naval Reserve officers. The first two are my former roommates aboard the *Lexington*: Richard Morland, PhD, who, during a long career as a professor at a Florida University, also established a reputation as a Naval historian. Richard Adelson, an antiquarian rare book dealer, has supplied me with out-of-print books on Naval histories. The third is my younger brother Rosario P. Romanelli, who, during the Korean War served as an Engineering Officer on the USS *Windham Bay,* a baby flattop, and who was later employed as President of Western Union International. All three used their extensive knowledge of U.S. Navy aircraft carriers to check my manuscript for errors; if any factual errors remain they are entirely my fault. Also any judgmental opinions are mine alone.

I owe thanks to my brother Marcello J. Romanelli, a Grumman design engineer, for the story of the Grumman "Iron Works" and Admiral McCain's remarks.

I also owe a debt of gratitude to my sister-in-law Lois Diane Hicks for her painstaking editing and for keyboarding my scribbles into my irascible and persnickety computer, whose unpredictable glitches are frequently frustrating.

Finally, I am indebted to my loving wife Dorothy, who, to quote some words from Samuel Eliot Morison, "... greatly contributed to my happiness and well being while the work was going on."

PREFACE

ABOUT THE BLUE GHOST

The "Blue Ghost" is a nickname, coined by Tokyo Rose, for the USS *Lexington* CV-16, an Essex class aircraft carrier. Starting in 1941, twenty-four carriers of this design were built. We are thankful to Franklin D. Roosevelt for his foresight in preparing the U.S. Navy for a conflict he saw was inevitable. In the 1930s he had to cajole Congress and wangle funds to get four carriers built: *Yorktown, Enterprise, Wasp,* and *Hornet.*

The existence of these four carriers plus *Lexington* CV-2 and *Saratoga* were the principal force that held the Japanese fleet in check for a year and a half until the *Essex* class carriers could start to arrive in the Pacific.

In 1941 the keel for an aircraft carrier to be named the *Cabot* was laid in a Bethlehem Steel shipyard in Quincy, Massachusetts. But in May of 1942, an aircraft carrier designated USS *Lexington* CV-2, commissioned in 1927, was sunk in the battle of the Coral Sea. CV-2 was the fourth naval vessel in U.S. Navy history to be named *Lexington*, commemorating the site of the first battle in the American Revolutionary War, when the Minute-men shed the first blood of the war.

When the news that *Lexington* CV-2 had been sunk reached the Boston area, the shipyard workmen building the *Cabot* petitioned the Secretary of the Navy Department to change the name *Cabot* to *Lexington* CV-16. The completed carrier was christened in February of 1943 with its new name.

Lexington CV-16 transited the Panama Canal and reached the central Pacific in the summer of 1943. We were assigned to a Task Group in Task Force 38, the "Fast Carrier Task Force" and immediately participated in raids against Japanese-held islands in the central Pacific. In one such action, retiring from a raid on the island of Kwajalien, an enemy torpedo bomber hit *Lexington* CV-16, leaving a gaping hole in the starboard stern and jamming the rudder in a sharp left-turn position. The damage required a return to Bremerton, Washington for repairs.

Of course the Japanese pilot reported that he had sunk the *Lexington* and Tokyo Rose announced in her radio broadcast that they had sunk the "Blue Ghost." She was referring to the fact that the Japanese Navy had sunk the previous *Lexington* (CV-2) and the new one (CV-16) now was the reincarnation ("Ghost"). The "Blue" was a reference to the color of our ship's faded coat of paint (the newer carriers sported grey coats of camouflage paint).

After being repaired in Bremerton, the ship returned to the fray in the central and western Pacific and Tokyo Rose "sank" us on another three occasions. Our crew laughed at Tokyo Rose and considered her reports a mark of honor and distinction.

Despite the torpedo hit, the Kamikaze hit and reports by Tokyo Rose of having been sunk on several different occasions, the "Blue Ghost" sailed into Tokyo Bay on September 2, 1945 to attend the surrender of the Japanese nation.

The Essex class carriers were the mainstay of the U.S. Navy's efforts to take back control of the Pacific Ocean from the Japanese Navy. Simultaneously with the attack on Pearl Harbor, the Japanese fleets started actions all over the central and western Pacific as far as the Indian Ocean, to subdue strategically important islands and destroy all naval warships and commercial shipping. For example, three days after the Pearl Harbor attack, their airplanes sank the British battleship *Prince of Wales* and the battle cruiser *Repulse* in the waters close to Singapore.

The Essex class carriers displaced 27,100 tons (standard), 36,380 tons loaded with fuel, supplies, ammunition and 100 airplanes. The flight deck was 872 feet long and 147 feet wide. The propulsion was four screws, 150,000 horsepower, maximum speed 34 knots. Complement, including air department, 3,500. Armament included four twin 5-inch 38 caliber turrets and four 5-inch singles; eighteen 40mm quad mounts and fifty-two 20mm AA guns.

In the number of airplanes, speed, armament and modern equipment, such as radars, the Essex class carriers were equal to, or superior to, the first-class carriers of the Japanese fleet. Furthermore, the 24 Essex class carriers built, outnumbered the Japanese 3 to 1. No Essex class carrier was ever sunk, though many sustained severe battle damage.

Lexington CV-16 compiled an impressive war record:

- 35 major battles. She steamed the equivalent of 7 times around the world (175,000 miles), all in the Pacific.
- Her air group destroyed 372 enemy planes in the air and 475 on the ground and 300,000 tons of shipping sunk or damaged.
- Her four air groups suffered losses of 169 pilots and crewmen.
- Her ships complement suffered losses of 59 dead and 167 wounded,from an enemy torpedo and Kamikaze.
- Presidential Unit Citation: one of only nine carriers to receive this award

The "Blue Ghost" USS Lexington CV-16, circa 1943. (Courtesy of Richand Morland)

CHAPTER 1

INTRODUCTION

During the late 1930s, when I was a teenager going to Stuyvesant High School in New York City, I used to take the Sea Beach Express to go from our home in Bay Ridge, Brooklyn to Manhattan. I would get off the subway train at Union Square, which, in those days, the mid-thirties, was a hot-bed of political discussion groups – Socialists, Communists and Pacifists. On the way home through the Square, some friends and I would occasionally stop to heckle the Pacifists. We had no respect for Pacifism. We knew from the law of the Bay Ridge streets that the best way to ensure peace and respect was with your fists. Pacifists were yellow cowards.

Later, while attending the Polytechnic Institute, I learned the history of European wars from Professor Emil Lengyel, a native of Hungary, who had observed European politics first hand during the early 1900s. From another on-the-scene observer, newspaper correspondent Upton Close, I heard about the rape of Manchuria by Japan in 1932. These accounts impressed me with the need to combat aggression and protect our precious freedom. To me, the march of Hitler and Tojo during this period was outrageous and carried with it dire forebodings. And so it was that the U.S. Navy made me an offer that I couldn't refuse: a commission in the Naval Reserve. In my youthful idealism, I would fight for freedom and participate in the exciting adventure of the coming conflict.

I was called to active duty on July 1, 1942, right after graduating with a degree in Mechanical Engineering. After a 60-day indoctrination course at Cornell University, where we marched around the campus, studied Navy Regulations and read about John Paul Jones, I was ordered to the Ordnance and Gunnery School at the Navy Yard in Washington, D.C. There, we learned about every type of Naval explosive weapons from pistols to battleship turrets. They were training us to be ordnance inspectors at armament factories across the country. But when it came time to graduate from the school, four of us decided we wanted sea duty and the Executive Officer was happy to oblige.

THE SECRETARY OF THE NAVY
WASHINGTON

The President of the United States takes pleasure in presenting the PRESIDENTIAL UNIT CITATION to the

U.S.S. LEXINGTON

and her attached Air Groups participating in the following operations:

September 18, 1943, Tarawa; October 5-6, 1943, Wake; November 19 to December 5, 1943, Gilberts: AG-16 (VF-16, VB-16, VT-16).

March 18 to April 30, 1944, Palau, Hollandia, Truk; June 11 to July 5, 1944, Marianas: AG-16 (VF-16, VB-16, VT-16, Part of VFN-76).

July 18 to August 5, 1944, Marianas, Palau, Bonins; September 6 to November 6, 1944, Philippines, Palau, Yap, Ryukyus, Formosa, Luzon: AG-19 (VF-19, VB-19, VT-19, Part of VFN-76).

December 14-16, 1944, Luzon; January 3 to 22, 1945, Philippines, Formosa, China Sea, Ryukyus: AG-20 (VF-20, VB-20, VT-20).

February 16 to March 1, 1945, Japan, Bonins, Ryukyus: AG-9 (VF-9, VBF-9, VB-9, VT-9).

June 20, 1945, Wake; July 10 to August 15, 1945, Japan: AG-94 (VF-94, VBF-94, VB-94, VT-94).

for service as set forth in the following

CITATION:

"For extraordinary heroism in action against enemy Japanese forces in the air, ashore and afloat in the Pacific War Area from September 18, 1943, to August 15, 1945. Spearheading our concentrated carrier-warfare in the most forward areas, the U.S.S. LEXINGTON and her air groups struck crushing blows toward annihilating Japanese fighting power; they provided air cover for our amphibious forces; they fiercely countered the enemy's aerial attacks and destroyed his planes; and they inflicted terrific losses on the Japanese in Fleet and merchant marine units sunk or damaged. Daring and dependable in combat, the LEXINGTON with her ga[illegible] officers and men rendered loyal service in achieving the ulti[illegible]e defeat of the Japanese Empire."

FITNESS
REPORTS

For the President,

Noted pers-101

James Forrestal
Secretary of the Navy

Presidential Unit Citation.

In 1926 I was a 6-year-old immigrant boy from Italy, born into an old culture and an ethnic group that had not yet earned respect in their adopted country. In 1942 I was about to embark on an adventure that would earn me my spurs and respect in the country I had embraced.

I was ordered to a pre-commissioning detail for an aircraft carrier being outfitted at a Boston shipyard, the USS *Lexington*, CV-16, an Essex-class design.

Of course, I had no idea of what I was getting into, but sea duty promised excitement and, after four years of intense engineering studies, I was ready for adventure.

In the course of this adventure, I was not a hero in the traditional sense. I followed orders and did my job to the best of my ability and good judgment. I earned the confidence of my superiors; two commanding officers entrusted me with the responsibilities of Officer of the Deck to conn the ship in the war zone; and, as a Division Officer I earned the respect of my men. I had a reputation of being "tough but fair," a description which, when filtered back to my usually phlegmatic father, made him stand a foot taller. I fulfilled my role as a team player and felt I had fully earned my share of the Presidential Unit Citation which was awarded to the *Lexington*.

The vignettes that follow are personal memoirs, all true accounts, according to my recollections, of feelings and occurrences, written in the tradition of James Michener's *Tales of the South Pacific*, which I admire. The events are a slice of Navy life during war time.

For anyone interested in a comprehensive history of the USS *Lexington* CV-16 please refer to the following:

1. *The History of U.S. Naval Operations in World War II*, Volumes 7, 8, 12, by Samuel Eliot Morison. Little Brown and Company 1951, '53, '58.
2. *The Blue Ghost*, by Edward Steichen. Harcourt Brace 1947.
3. *USS Lexington CV/CVS/CVT-16.* Turner Publishing Company, Paducah, Kentucky.
4. *Tarawa To Tokyo*, published by the officers and men of the USS *Lexington.*
5. *Aircraft Carriers*, by Norman Polmar. Published in Japan 1969
6. *Carrier War*, by Lt. Oliver Jensen, USNR. Pocket Books, Inc., N.Y. 1945.

In recent years I have been indebted to these books for certain dates and events of which I had not been previously aware. My feelings and judgments, particularly regarding Admiral William "Bull" Halsey, are my own. As far as the rest of the Navy is concerned, I hold a deep respect, admiration and a warm feeling of brotherhood and family.

In addition to the above, I want to add the names of two more books recommended by an authoritative source. These authors served on the *Lexington* at the same time and their personal accounts make for interesting reading.

Mission Beyond Darkness, by Bryan J. and Philip Read. Duell, Sloan and Pearce 1945.

Skipper: Confessions of a Fighter Squadron Commander, 1943-1944, by T. Hugh Winters. Mesa, Arizona.

CHAPTER 2

CAPTAIN FELIX STUMP

Felix Stump was a graduate of the Naval Academy class of 1917. His duty assignments included: Navigator, USS *Cincinnati* in World War I, flight training, aeronautical engineering, squadron Commanding Officer, Navigator, *Lexington* CV2 1936-37, Executive Officer, *Enterprise* 1940-41, Commanding Officer, *Langley* 1941. This prior experience provided eminent qualifications for the very prestigious assignment as Commissioning Captain of a new aircraft carrier during World War II.

In that war, the aircraft carrier was replacing the battleship as the most formidable warship of all time.

Among the additional qualifications needed for such an assignment were the fitness report recommendations of previous superior officers certifying that Felix was highly qualified to command a naval vessel, a role that required intelligence, experience, courage, high standards, leadership, and political savvy. In short, Plato's Philosopher King. He was to demonstrate these qualities in full measure during the next three years as Commanding Officer of the USS *Lexington* and Admiral of a fleet of escort carriers.

My first contact with Stump occurred on the day after the *Lexington* was commissioned in February of 1943. The ship was tied to a pier at the Boston Navy Yard in the process of fitting out. The commissioning crew had moved aboard the day before and I learned that I had been assigned the duty as Junior Officer of the Deck (JOOD) for the 0800 to noon watch the next morning. I reported to the quarterdeck, a roped-off section of the hangar deck adjacent to the gangway and asked the OOD, Lieut. Nickerson what I was supposed to do. He replied, "Stick close and you will soon find out."

The primary activity was watching the civilian navy yard workers coming aboard with their tools and supplies. We had to check their identification badges, as part of our job was to protect the ship from saboteurs. I had a 45-caliber semi-automatic pistol strapped to my waist but had not been instructed on how or under what circumstances to use it.

Captain Felix Stump

Toward the middle of the watch, the Bosun mate rushed over to Nickerson and said that an admiral was coming aboard. Nickerson and I rushed to the gangway to receive him and stood at ramrod-stiff attention. The admiral wanted to see the captain. Nickerson turned to me and said, "Escort the admiral to the captain's cabin." I whispered, "Where is the captain's cabin?" He replied, "Up in the gallery deck. Go up that ladder then turn inboard."

The gallery deck was a maze of catwalks, hung below the flight deck and leading athwartship and fore and aft. After several turns of catwalks, I could see no cabin and I was reduced to having to ask directions from a yard workman, of all indignities!

After I finally saw the admiral through the door of the captain's cabin, I heard him laugh and say, "Felix, you have your work cut out for you with this green crew. Your JOOD doesn't even know where your cabin is." Needless to say, I was embarrassed; I had failed my first assignment. When I got back to the quarterdeck I told Nickerson we were in trouble.

About half an hour later, the captain and the admiral came down the ladder. After he saw the admiral over the side, Stump approached us. He was a very tall, imposing figure, who stooped slightly when he was talking to people who were shorter than he was.

I was standing one step behind and one step to the side of Nickerson but Stump never looked at me or spoke to me directly. His remarks were all directed to Nickerson. Stump was following the chain of command.

In a cold, deliberate tone, with neither humor nor histrionics, he instructed Nickerson as to how the OOD should instruct a green JOOD on his duties. "Know the ship like the back of your hand; maintain order and discipline; be prepared to assume all the duties of the OOD; etc., etc." When he had finished, he turned on his heels and without delay he quickly proceeded up the ladder to his cabin. Nickerson turned to me and said, "See, now you know what to do around here."

Such was my first encounter with our first captain, whose leadership I came to respect and be thankful for in times of crisis in future years.

CHAPTER 3

SHAKEDOWN

After months of outfitting, tuning equipment, loading supplies and ammunition, and assembling the crew, it was time for sea trials. It was time to test the ship and all its equipment and start training the crew to perform its duties under various conditions. Of course, the most critical operation was flight operations, including pilot training. The great day finally arrived. We were putting out to sea for our shakedown cruise.

It was a busy morning and I had worked up an appetite, so I ate a hearty lunch of curried chicken and rice. We left Boston Harbor, rounded the northernmost tip of Cape Cod, the town of Provincetown and once in the open waters of the Atlantic Ocean headed smack into a hurricane.

We headed south with several escorting destroyers. Our cruising speed normally would have been 18 knots but the destroyers were taking green water down their stacks, so we slowed down to 10 knots. The slower speed only served to aggravate the roll and pitch of the ship and we had not yet developed our sea legs.

My station for the 1200 to 1600 watch was down in the bowels of the ship – the Fire Control Plot, which contained the Mark 1 Computer which computed the positioning parameters for the 5"/38 caliber guns.

This location was close to the center of gravity of the 36,000-ton USS *Lexington* and would normally experience the minimum movement in a storm. Because of the storm, we had a bucket at the ready and I kept eyeing it, as the curried chicken was giving me a queasy feeling in my stomach. I was also keeping an eye on my computer crew, which I felt was looking at me in a half-expectant manner. The crew consisted of a First Class Firecontrolman and four or five 17 and 18 year old "green," landlubber sailors.

I was the only officer (also a landlubber) and it was our first watch together. What was going on was a test of our resistance to sea-sickness and I had to set the proper example. Besides, I had to save face!

Who would be the first to use the bucket? It was one of the longest four-hour watches I ever experienced. I watched the clock and each minute seemed like an hour. Finally my relief arrived, I had survived the bucket test. But not quite fully, for I had to climb up from the 7th deck to the 3rd deck, up four ladders and through man-holes in four hatches before I could get to an officers head.

My lunch was surging up in my gullet. I reached the third deck and started running down the passageway to the head (toilet) I knew was close to the wardroom ... Before I got there, the Gunnery Officer, Cdr. North., my superior, appeared in front of me and said, "Rummy, I want to ask you ..."

"Sorry sir, but I have an urgent call in the head."

So I made it to the toilet and disgorged my lunch and part of my breakfast too. I spent the next 24 hours in my bunk, except for watch duty. An empty stomach is no protection against the impulse to heave your guts out. But it was the first and only time in 2 1/2 years and four typhoons that I was seasick. During that time I found my sea legs and my stomach behaved.

On the way south to the Gulf of Paria, off the South American coast, we stopped off at Norfolk, Virginia. We anchored in the Hampton Roads, where the water was deep enough to accommodate our deep-draft hull. Our anchorage was about 5 miles from the Fleet Landing where our small boats had to convey our liberty parties.

I found my name on the list of Boat Officers to man the liberty boats.

"My only experience with small boats was with a rowboat in Central Park."

"That's okay, you'll have an experienced coxswain to pilot the boat."

"Then why do you need me?"

"We have to have an officer to take the rap in case the boat sinks."

Fortunately we did not sink. But when we reached the crowded fleet landing, my coxswain proved his inexperience; he kept bumping into other boats, to my embarrassment. After bumping a captain's gig and an admiral's barge, I decided I could do no worse, so I took the tiller and assigned him to "bump control," with an oar to ease any contact with other boats. On our return trip, I was apprehensive about the approaching darkness and our ability to find the ship. Fortunately we completed the trying mission without further ado.

The next day it was my turn to go ashore on liberty, this time as a passenger, not as a boat officer, thank God. Prior to going ashore, I put on my Dress Whites in the bunkroom I shared with my friend Richard Adelson. He wasn't going ashore, he was ship-bound with communications duty.

Joshing with Dick about drinking ashore, I said, "Should I order us a couple of cool Tom Collins?" As a tease, I picked up the ship's phone and dialed 000, knowing that that number was not listed as being assigned to any compartment on the ship. I said, "This is Ensign Romanelli in JO Bunkroom number one. Please send up two Tom Collins' on the double!" Dick gave a reluctant laugh at my sense of humor, since he would have to wait for another day to savor a drink.

I went ashore as a passenger on the boat, savoring the relief of responsibility. I traipsed around Norfolk, where there were signs in some neighborhoods that said, "No dogs or sailors allowed," not exactly a welcoming greeting on behalf of the natives. I had a couple of Tom Collins' and then returned to the ship.

Along the passageway I passed the Executive Officer, Cdr. Sutcliffe, "Evening Sir," "Hi Rummy," and he gave me a broad grin, which he had never done before. When I reached the bunkroom, Dick was there and said, "Boy are you in hot water!"

"What for?"

"Well, your telephone order for the Tom Collins' went out over the bullhorn and was heard loud and clear by the Admiral of the Atlantic fleet in his command ship tied up on the opposite side of the mooring. He called our exec and wanted to know who Ensign Romanelli was. Our exec explained that 000 was an unlisted emergency number which you knew nothing about. He told him it was a boyish prank. Boy, you're going to get it!"

"Yeah, so that's why he smiled."

The Gulf of Paria is a large, protected body of water off the northern coast of South America. Access from the Atlantic Ocean was limited, so conducting flight operations was safe from German submarines.

Most of the pilots in Squadron 16 had not flown off a carrier before. As a consequence, there were numerous mishaps both on landings and take-offs. A total of 25 airplanes were lost but fortunately most of the pilots were saved by destroyers that were following us.

On the trip back north to Boston, the ship had to undergo speed trials. We achieved close to our design speed of 34 knots but not without the fantail trying to shake itself off from the rest of the ship.

Back in the Boston shipyard for "tune-up" repairs that turned up and the traditional ship's dance before "shipping out" to the war zone, we came to certain realizations.

First of all was the feeling of having survived our first cruise. For most members of the crew it was their first ocean cruise. We were "Old

Salts" and we could swagger down the Boston Common with our hats at a jaunty angle. We were getting accustomed to our new home and establishing a feeling of camaraderie with our shipmates.

Navy Regulations specifies that alcohol is not permitted on board naval vessels except under the charge of the medical officer, who can dispense it on an individual basis under special circumstances.

But a 17-year-old apprentice seaman would go ashore on liberty and get drunk to follow the traditional Navy image of the macho seaman. He would return to the ship and walk up the gangplank with that glassy-eyed smug look which said, "Today I am a sailor," as he saluted the flag and requested permission to come aboard. If he was carrying a bottle of booze, the OOD had to confiscate it and drop it over the side under the forlorn gaze of the besotted sailor.

On one occasion, in a U.S. port, the name of which I can't recall, I received word that two of my fire controlmen were in the local hoosegow and I had to go ashore to get them released. I assumed a fatherly demeanor (although I was only about 22 years old at the time). "They are good boys, having a little relaxation before shoving off tomorrow morning to face the Japanese bombs and torpedoes. Don't begrudge them a little fun. They may not come back from the war. Release them in my charge and I will make sure I get them back to the ship to sleep it off. If there are any fines to pay I will pay them out of my own pocket."

"No, that won't be necessary Lieutenant."

Out of the hoosegow: "That was a cheap lesson you guys got. Keep your noses clean in the future."

"Aye, Aye Sir."

But there were also some sobering thoughts. We had to survive the fury of the sea. The hurricane was a harbinger of the Pacific Ocean typhoons to come, the fury of which were to sink destroyers.

We were also concerned about the hazards of flight operations on take-offs and landings and losing aircraft and pilots. These hazards, intermingled with battles with the enemy, the consequences of which we could only imagine, preyed on our minds. We could only hope that when our time came we would acquit ourselves honorably. That "test" would come soon enough.

CHAPTER 4

INTO THE PACIFIC

In the first six months after bombing Pearl Harbor, the Japanese fleet had run wild and unopposed through the Central and Western Pacific and into the Indian Ocean. They had taken the Philippines, New Guinea, the Solomons, the Marshalls and Gilberts, Singapore, Malaysia and Burma.

With our battleships lying in the mud of Pearl Harbor and only three first-line carriers available, there wasn't very much the U.S. Navy could do to stop the Japanese juggernaut. But in April of 1942, when the USS *Hornet* CV-8 carried sixteen U.S. Army Air Force B-25s to within 650 miles of the Japanese coast and the B-25s bombed Tokyo, it made the Japanese nation sit up and take notice.

The Japanese had bombed airfields on the coast of Australia earlier but their thrust south to Australia in May 1942 was thwarted by *Lexington* CV-2 and *Yorktown*; at our expense, we lost the *Lexington* CV-2 and the *Yorktown* was severely damaged but made it back to Pearl Harbor for repairs.

In late May of 1942, Admiral Chester Nimitz received word from radio interceptions, of Japanese plans to attack Midway Island, a key base between Hawaii and Japanese-held islands to the west. He had only two first-line carriers available to protect Midway, the *Enterprise* and the *Hornet*. The *Yorktown*, which had just returned from the battle of the Coral Sea, needed three months to repair its damages. The Admiral needed the carrier to be ready in two days to assist in the defense of Midway.

An army of 1500 navy yard workmen poured over the *Yorktown* and two and one half days later she sailed out of Pearl Harbor to join the *Enterprise* and the *Hornet* to defend Midway against the Japanese invasion armada.

In the Midway battle, the three carriers, under Admirals Spruance and Fletcher, engaged the invasion armada, which consisted of the core group of four fleet carriers, several light carriers, eleven battleships and many cruisers and destroyers. Our airplanes sank all four fleet carriers, the loss of which so devastated Admiral Yamamoto that he called off the assault on Midway even though his remaining forces could have overwhelmed our meager forces.

In the engagement, we lost the spunky, damaged *Yorktown* to a submarine torpedo. Four-for-one was a satisfactory return.

The victory at Midway was the turning point in the Pacific war, the high-water mark of the Japanese eastern perimeter. The pre-war U.S. carriers had proven their mettle; in the summer and fall of 1942, the three remaining pre-war carriers in the Pacific – *Enterprise*, *Hornet*, *Saratoga* – were joined by the *Wasp*, transferred from the Atlantic fleet. The four could now conduct single-carrier hit-and-run strikes on selected Japanese outposts without fear of the now diminished force of Japanese carriers.

When the decision was made in Washington to stop the advance of Japanese land forces in the Solomon Islands, the Navy was tasked with the support of the U.S. Marines on Guadalcanal. In a series of brutal actions in October of 1942, we lost the *Hornet* and *Wasp* to enemy torpedoes while both the *Enterprise* and *Saratoga* were severely damaged.

At one point, with the *Saratoga* in drydock, the *Enterprise*, in between repairs, was the only available U.S. carrier in the Pacific. But the enemy lost one carrier, two battleships and eleven transports loaded with invasion troops. The loss of the battleships and transports convinced the enemy high command to abandon their efforts to dislodge the U.S. Marines and their progress in the Solomons was turned back.

In overall command of our forces in the Solomons campaign was Admiral William "Bull" Halsey; his aggressive leadership in stopping the Japanese advance earned him a promotion to 4-star Admiral.

It was not until the summer of 1943, when the *Enterprise* and *Saratoga* were joined with the new wave of Essex-class carriers and new light carriers (CVL's) and screening battleships, cruisers and destroyers, that our multi-carrier Task Groups, the Fast Carrier Task Forces, could range with impunity through the Marshall and Gilbert Islands, looking for a fight with the full strength of the Japanese Navy.

Lexington departed Boston in June of 1943, sailed down the East Coast and transited the Panama Canal. While waiting to transit, we anchored overnight in Colon to remove a gun sponson on our starboard side which could not fit through the Canal locks. In a liberty in Colon we marveled at an erotic performance of a one-man act entitled, "Beauty and the Beast" at a local nightclub.

Entering the Pacific Ocean, we enjoyed the calm, balmy climate of the tropical waters, so much more friendly than the stormy North Atlantic.

Little did we know at the time of the impending fury of the Pacific typhoons that awaited us.

We had to stop at San Francisco to pick up a battalion of Marines we were to transport to Hawaii. We took the liberty to spend a night at the St. Francis Hotel. The multi-tiered bunk-bed accommodations for the Marines on our hangar deck were not as luxurious as the St. Francis.

During the two-week passage to Hawaii we conducted drills and received additional training. We learned the quickest route from our bunks to our battle stations when the alarm bells clanged and "General Quarters. Man your battle stations" sounded, along with, "This is a drill." We arrived at Oahu in August of 1943. The great news was the wonderful victory of the *Enterprise*, *Hornet* and *Yorktown* (RIP) at the Battle of Midway.

We spent several weeks in Pearl Harbor for replenishment, repairs and a final tune-up before sailing westward into the war zone. We were awed, angered and chagrined at the sight of the battered and sunken battleships from the Japanese attacks twenty months earlier. If any of us needed proof of "the day of infamy," or needed strengthening of our resolve, a quick glance at the devastation of "battleship row" was all that was needed.

While waiting for yard workmen to get the ship ready, we toured the island of Oahu. We swam and surf-boarded the waters of Waikiki Beach, being careful not to get scratched by the barbed wire which was intended to impede a Japanese invasion. We were not impressed by the beach; Jones Beach on Long Island, New York, was much nicer.

While there in Oahu, I was assigned to two training sessions. One was held at the pistol range, the other at a fire-fighting facility, both ashore on the island. There were no earmuffs available at the pistol range and as a consequence, I was deaf for three days after I ended my training there.

At the fire-fighting facility there was a two-story steel structure approximately 20 feet square which had no doors. The only access was through a hatch opening in the roof and another on the second deck.

They had started a fire with oily rags that filled the whole building with dense smoke. There was another fire in a pool of oil, which we had to extinguish.

We had a crew of six people and as I was the only officer, I was handed the heavy brass nozzle at the end of a 2-inch hose. Since they only had enough breathing masks for my crew, I was to be the "smoke-eater."

From the roof, I could see the vertical steel ladder extending down from the hatch to the second deck. I could feel the location of the second hatch but the dense smoke obscured the location of the second ladder.

Assuming the second ladder was to be found in the same location as the first, I put one leg down into the hatch, probing for the top rung of the ladder. The ladder was not there. Instead, I fell through the hatch down to the first deck, still holding the nozzle, which helped break my fall.

We put out the blaze and got our fire-fighting certificates. My 21-year-old body recovered from the smoke inhalation and several bruises.

At the bar in the Royal Hawaiian Hotel in Honolulu, we picked up a couple of apocryphal stories making the rounds at that time. One story concerned a lieutenant supply officer who was onboard a destroyer that was torpedoed and was sinking. Before abandoning ship, he emptied his safe of over one million dollars in large-denomination bills and packed them in a water-tight bag which he carried overboard.

He was picked up by another destroyer and he offered the money to the supply officer there who didn't know how to account for it and therefore refused to accept it. Ashore at Pearl Harbor the authorities also refused to accept the money.

At the 13th Naval District in San Francisco, they wired Washington asking for instructions. The word came back, "All assets of the ship were written off when it sank. We have no rights to the money."

When asked by friends who knew his story, what he was doing with the money, his answer was, "It's in a bank account. If the government ever decides it wants the principal, I'll return that and keep the interest."

Another apocryphal story had to do with a young ensign who was apprehended by the shore patrol because he was stark naked and chasing a young woman down a hallway at the Royal Hawaiian Hotel. He was court-martialed for being out of uniform. His smart attorney got him acquitted with the argument that he was "dressed for the sport."

While still in Honolulu I ran into a boyhood chum who used to live across the street from our apartment in Bay Ridge, Brooklyn; a little bit of nostalgia 6,000 miles away from home. So much for the tourist interlude.

We came to fight!

The *Lexington* was assigned to Task Group 50.1 along with the new *Yorktown* (CV10) and new light carrier *Cowpens* (CVL-25). This group started conducting aircraft strikes in September on Marcus, Tarawa and Makin Islands. In November we struck Jaluit and Mili in the Marshall Islands.

We received mail from home via Fleet Post Office. My mother would bake hard cookies, which, many years later, my daughter dubbed the "one-two" cookies because of the number of chocolate bits in each. The cookies were a welcome treat from home which I shared with my roommates.

My roommate Dick also received packages from home. His family owned a candy factory and his packages bore the name of the factory and the contents were labeled as "chocolate syrup." In fact, the packages contained a bottle of Haig and Haig Pinch, a fine Scotch.

Our room had a wall safe which was to be used to safeguard classified documents but the only time the safe was locked was when it contained Haig and Haig Pinch. Of course our friends were always on the lookout for "chocolate syrup," for that meant a party of "one-two" cookies and Haig and Haig Pinch.

The "tip-off" on when we expected action from the enemy came in the morning when we were fed a "battle breakfast" of steak and eggs. For the rest of the day and maybe the following night the meals consisted of just Spam sandwiches. The sandwiches weren't bad but trying to rest at night on a steel deck while wearing telephones and steel helmets during general quarters was not very comfortable.

In the wardroom, the food wasn't bad if you could tolerate powdered eggs and orange macaroni. The biggest shortage was in fresh fruits and vegetables and milk. If you complained about the mess service you were likely to be shackled with the responsibility of being the mess officer, as happened to Marine Captain Rich; he sure made the mess boys snap to attention.

I recall my first meal ashore on our first return to Bremerton: a lettuce and tomato sandwich, a shot of bourbon and a glass of milk.

CHAPTER 5

FIRE CONTROL

Because of my engineering education and Navy courses in ordnance and gunnery, I was assigned to the Lexington's Eighth (Fire Control) Division as a junior officer. In Navy parlance, "Fire Control" refers to aiming and controlling gunfire. Fire fighting is the primary responsibility of the damage control group of the hull department, though of course every person on board must help in extinguishing a blaze.

8th Division Officer Lt. Ralph Jones, was my immediate superior. When he was transferred for medical reasons, I was assigned that responsibility. As Division Officer I had to be a "father" to about 150 Fire Controlmen, Torpedomen, gunnersmates and the Gunnery Dept. yoeman.

The third deck of the ship was where most of the divisional offices were located. It was like a mall, where your CPO or divisional leading petty officer went shopping for divisional material needs and service. The barter system was the trading style – an electric motor for a gallon of paint, or some kind of political favor.

Our armory held a collection of firearms – pistols, rifles, 30 and 50-caliber machine guns and ammunition. A competent 1st class gunnersmate, a little more mature than our 17-year-old sailors was in charge.

He returned to the ship after a two-week leave in Kentucky and greeted me like a long-lost buddy. The glazed look in his eyes and his ruddy complexion indicated that he had been drinking but I couldn't smell any alcohol on his breath. I accused him of being drunk, which he did not deny and he offered me a small bottle of 120-proof "good ole Kentucky moonshine."

Of course I declined his offer and said that furthermore I would confiscate his supply. But he wouldn't tell me where he was hiding it. I gave him 24 hour to sober up, or I would put him on report. He complied.

Our primary purpose was to select targets and direct the firing of the 5-inch, 40mm and 20mm guns, including the alignment and maintenance of the associated equipment.

Equipment for the 5-inch guns included two Mark 37 Directors, located fore and aft of the island structure. The directors sighted the targets and tracked them visually or by special radar. The director crew consisted of a Director Officer, two trackers with telescopes; one in azimuth, the other in elevation, a radar operator to track range and an optical rangefinder operator for target identification and stereoscopic range measurement as a backup to the radar range measurement.

The director's measurement of target, bearing, elevation and range was transmitted electrically to a Computer Mark 1 in Fire Control Plot deep in the bowels of the ship, on the seventh deck. The Mark 1 Computer, a pre-war development, was housed in a steel box about 8 feet long, 4 feet wide and 3 $^1/_2$ feet high. It is an electromechanical marvel of precision analog devices that can add, subtract, multiply, differentiate and integrate. There is a three-dimensional steel cam roughly the shape of a large ocarina that has been machined to simulate ballistic data like superelevation, which compensates for the effect of gravity on the path of the projectile.

The computer receives the parameters of the target's present position (bearing, elevation, range) from the director, computes the rates of change of these parameters, multiplies these rates of change by the estimated time of flight of the projectile to the target's future range and arrives at the parameters of future target position, then adds superelevation to allow for the projectile's trajectory and applies a wind correction to establish an Aim Point.

Finally, to compensate for the movement of the ship in roll and pitch, the computer receives instantaneous readings of the ship's roll and pitch angles from the master gyro from the compartment adjacent to Fire Control Plot.

All of the above computations are necessary when you consider the problem of trying to hit a fast-moving aircraft five or six miles away from an unstable platform. There is one additional aid to scoring a hit and that comes with a magnetic sensing device in the nose of a 5-inch projectile, called an influence type fuse. With this projectile you can miss the target by 15 feet and still score a hit.

The final parameters of the aim point are transmitted electrically through a massive switchboard to the gun mounts that have been selected by Gunnery Control to do the firing.

I was fortunate to have had the opportunity to study the guts of a Computer Mark 1 at the Brooklyn Navy Yard during the summer of 1941 when I was ordered to training duty. Because of this training I was assigned to

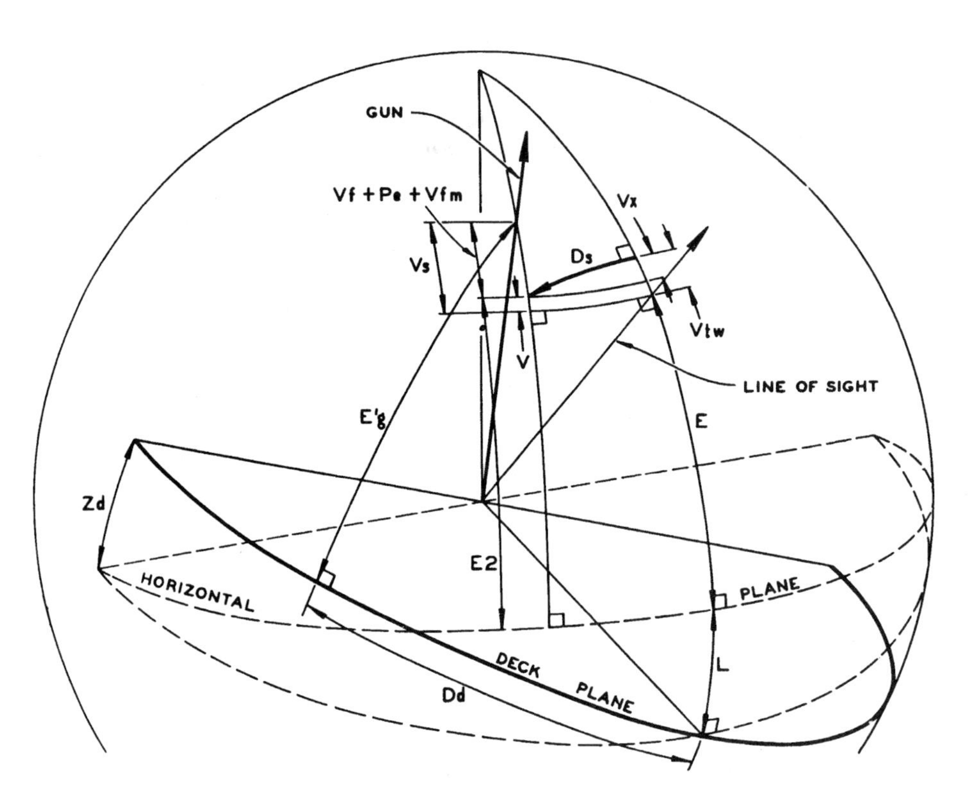

Computer MK.1, MOD. 1 to 7
Spherical Diagram of Anti-aircraft problem

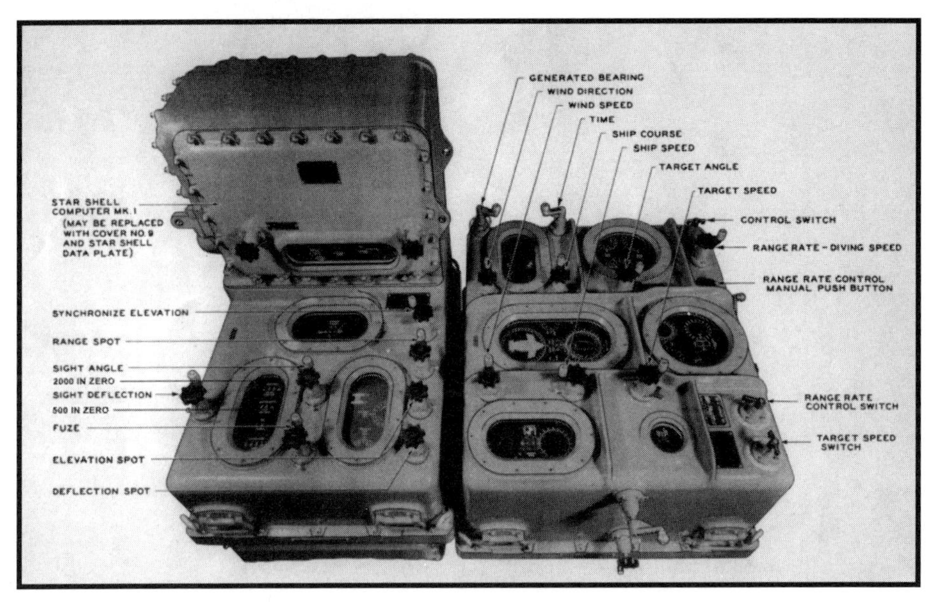

Computer MK.1, MOD. 4,7
Top

Computer MK.1, MOD. 7
Front right view, covers removed

AA Batteries aft of Island, F6F coming in for landing.

40mm Fire Control men, part of the 8th Division.

train our computer crews on board the "*Lex.*" The crew members were 17, 18 and 19-year-olds but were all very bright young men. Rated Fire Controlmen are technically the brightest rating on the ship, requiring basic knowledge of physics, electricity, mathematics, optics and radar.

In teaching operators of the Mark 1 Computer, I sought to give them a sense of the different devices performing different functions. We had a First Class Fire Controlman who was in charge of Fire Control Plot. He was a taciturn individual but he knew the Mark 1 like the back of his hand. When I was trying to explain the computer to the new crews, he stood in the background leaning against the bank of switching controls not saying a word except for an occasional caustic, "That ain't right." It was embarrassing to me, not only because it revealed the limits of my knowledge but also because it offended my sense of authority.

I was sure that what he was thinking was, "What does this snot-nosed Ensign know about my computer? I'll show him a thing or two." This went on until I finally had to tell him to put up (teach the crew) or shut up. He chose the latter.

I later recommended him for promotion to Chief Petty Officer. Some years later, talking with some former instructors at the Fire Control School in Washington, D.C., I learned that Chief Wright had been the bane of the instructors there with his caustic, "That ain't right," in the middle of a lecture.

I like to think that my teaching efforts did some good. In one of our first attacks by three enemy torpedo planes in the Marshall and Gilbert Islands, our 5-inch fire control team splashed two planes at a range of about five thousand yards and assisted the 40mm and 20mm batteries in splashing the other attacker. Our fire control team had proved its mettle to the entire ship's company. "Well done."

This success was particularly gratifying because since we were in the center of the formation and the attacking planes had to pass over the circle of screening destroyers and then battleships and cruisers, we were the only ship to fire on the attackers. The attackers were aiming at the Blue Ghost.

Our 40mm batteries were controlled by separate Directors placed in close proximity to the guns.

The 20mm guns were outfitted with a lead-computing sight mounted on the gun cradle. The lead-computing sight contained a small gyroscope whose precession provided the lead angle when tracking a moving target. The gunsight was developed at MIT by Doctor Draper, who was later awarded the Victory Medal for his accomplishments by President Kennedy.

This is one more example of the superior technology that gave our ships advantage over the Japanese equipment.

Along these same lines, I would be remiss if I did not acknowledge our debt to the array of specialized ship's radar sets that provided our fire control system with the advance warning and location of incoming enemy planes before they closed within effective range of our gun batteries.

These specialized radars were able to detect the approach of a massive airborne attack by Japanese planes from a distance of 150 miles while Task Force 58 was charged with protecting the landing forces at Saipan. This advance warning enabled our Combat Air Patrol to pounce on the 450-plane attacking force from an altitude of 20,000 feet and to destroy more than 400 aircraft in the famous "Marianas Turkey Shoot."

Special radars were indispensible in aircraft fighter-direction and for navigation and station-keeping at night. One of these special radars was a height-finding (elevation measurement) radar designated as the CXBL, experimental radar. We received this equipment during the outfitting period in Boston. At the same time, the developer of this equipment, a physicist, by the name of Bob Hensell reported aboard to install and maintain the equipment.

On a Friday afternoon in February of 1943, at the electronics laboratory at John Hopkins University in Maryland, he had packed the equipment for shipment. On the following Monday he arrived in Boston in a brand new, ill-fitting, Navy uniform to unpack and install his "baby" on the top-most platform of our superstructure. Which, incidentally, also became his General Quarters battle station, where, armed with a screwdriver and plyers, his job was to keep the CXBL operating.

He and I became friends and took our evening constitutional on the flight deck counting stars and discussing philosophy.

The 8th Division was also responsible for the magazines which stored bombs, torpedoes and other ammunition. An optical shop which serviced 20mm gunsights and an armory which maintained machine guns, rifles and pistols was another part of the 8th Division, as were the Torpedo Shop and the Torpedomen ratings which serviced the aerial torpedoes to be ready to mount on torpedo planes attacking enemy surface ships.

Some 5-inch projectiles came with influence-type fuses, which were classified confidential. This classification required that each shipment be counted by an officer to assure that none had been lost or absconded with during transit.

The projectiles were hoisted aboard by crane and laid out on the flight deck. The counting had to be done by moving each projectile from one pile to another by a working party of seamen. Each projectile weighed about 60 pounds, a vigorous weight-lifting exercise.

Since a typical shipment consisted of several thousand projectiles, each member of the 10-man working party would have to lift and carry several hundred projectiles. When I had the counting duty, I had to make sure to count carefully, because if my tally did not match the shipping manifest the pile would have to be recounted by moving it to another pile. I dreaded the prospect of having to tell a weary working party to move 60 tons of projectiles a second time.

All explosives were stored deep in the bowels of the ship, surrounded by nonflammable sea water or fresh water ballast tanks. When they were needed by airplanes or guns, the bombs, torpedoes and projectiles were brought topside by special armament elevators.

500 and 1000-pound bombs were usually hoisted aboard when the ship was alongside a pier. On one occasion, during a raid on Palau it was necessary to replenish a load of 500-pound bombs at open sea, from an ammunition barge.

The barge was tied alongside the ship with bumpers in between them to prevent direct contact with the ship's hull. The sea was relatively smooth but long swells raised and lowered the barge independently from the effect they had on the ship's movement. The barge bobbed up and down alongside the ship.

I had a working party in the hull of the barge. Our job was to attach a cradle to each bomb and move it to a position beneath the open hatch and hook it, with plenty of slack, to the cable from the ship's crane. The trickiest part was to take up the slack on the cable when the vertical position of the barge was at its lowest point with respect to the ship and from that point, taking up slack as the barge is rising. At the top of its rise, the crane operator is signalled to hoist as quickly as possible to clear the hatch opening.

With proper coordination we were able to avoid having the bombs being bounced on the deck of the barge. Of course we knew that the bombs had no fuses and therefore would not explode if bumped or dropped. Even so, we were relieved when we had to discontinue the operation because of a submarine scare in the vicinity.

The chief torpedoman was a very experienced, grey-haired warrant officer, in whom I had the utmost confidence. (This comment also applies to the other warrant officers and CPO's in my division; they knew their job and did it and I never had occasion to question their judgment.)

The torpedomen's job was to service the torpedoes periodically so that they would function satifactorily when dropped by the torpedo bombers. Though I had heard reports of some torpedoes not exploding when striking the hull of an enemy ship, I was not aware of any such reports from pilots from our ship.

There was one mishap in the torpedo shop however, that was quite alarming to those who were present in the shop at the time.

The explosive warhead was stored separately from the fuse and from the main body which housed the propulsion engine. These components were transferred between the shop and storage magazines by a hoist which lifted or lowered the component through hatches in each deck level.

One day they were lowering a warhead from the third deck to the seventh, when the harness broke loose from the warhead; it fell, striking the hatch coamings of each deck on the way down. When it finally struck the seventh deck, it split open and spilled the explosive on the deck. Fortunately there was no fuse in the warhead and the explosive was Torpex, the safest explosive available.

Now each torpedoman knew that the warhead was not supposed to explode but watching that warhead bounce from hatch coaming to hatch coaming and then splitting apart on the seventh deck was a horror show sufficient to turn one's hair grey.

Perhaps that was how Chief Torpedoman Hopkins got his grey hair.

CHAPTER 6

TORPEDO

During September, October and November of 1943, *Lexington* planes participated in air strikes on atolls or islands in the Marshall and Gilbert Islands. We on board ship would watch the planes roar off and we awaited their return with expectations of hearing about their successes. We participated vicariously in their successful attacks. We were the "home folks," taking care of their base operations.

At the beginning of the war, the Japanese "Zero," Mitsubishi A6M5, was the undisputed master of the Pacific skies. It was faster and more maneuverable than our F4F Wildcat. In early 1942 a Zero in good condition was captured in the Aleutians and immediately rushed to Grumman Aircraft Company on Long Island, New York so that they could satisfy the request of "Butch" O'Hare for "Something that will go upstairs faster."

The Naval Bureau of Aeronautics ordered Grumman to put the Zero through its paces and then design a fighter that was its superior in every way and to do it fast! The Grumman engineers did themselves proud. Their F6F had more power, speed, 50-caliber machine guns, self-sealing gas tanks and more protection for the pilot. Because of the steel armor plate with which they surrounded the pilot they renamed their factory "The Iron Works." The first F6F was flown in August of 1942.

In appreciation, Vice Admiral John McCain visited Long Island to tell the Grumman engineers and factory workers that "The Grumman name on an airplane has the same meaning to the Navy as the name Sterling on silver has to you." At that time McCain was Chief of the Bureau of Aeronautics. Later, he succeeded Admiral Mitscher as Commander of the Fast Carrier Task Force and, still later, he fathered the current Senator from Arizona who bears his name.

A year later the fighter pilots now had the Grumman F6F's, the new masters of the Pacific skies and they took full advantage of their new equipment. Quite a few pilots became "instant aces," having shot down five or more Zeros in a single engagement; they established a kill ratio of

F6F Grumman "Hellcat" ready for take-off.

nine to one. We on board ship were proud of them, as if they were our precocious kid brothers. But that "home-body" passive role started to change.

On the morning of December 4, 1943, our task group launched large strikes against Kwajalein, Wotje Atolls and Roi Island. The enemy was caught by surprise and our planes shot down many enemy airplanes and sank an ammunition ship. Since that area was a hornet's nest of land-based aircraft we decided to retire eastward out of range of these airplanes, as soon as we recovered our planes.

But about noon, six "Kate" torpedo planes found our task group and attacked our formation. Three planes selected the *Lexington.* Lt.jg John Crane, USNR, was the Director Officer in the forward Mk 37 Director, controlling the five-inch battery. He and his director crew spotted three low-flying Kate torpedo planes at about 7,000 yards as they were passing over the destroyer screen. He reported the sighting to Gunnery Control, requesting permission to commence firing. Not receiving an immediate reply and with the Kates rapidly approaching, he issued the firing order on his own initiative. The 5-inch guns shot down the first two Kates and wounded the third, which was finished off by the 40mm guns.

John was fearful of being reprimanded for firing without permission but he was reassured by his division officer Lt. Wells, who gave him a "Well Done"! John Crane was later awarded a Silver Star medal for his initiative.

This was the first attack against our ship and we were jubilant that our ship's guns had proved their mettle. The other three Kates attacked the new *Yorktown* and they also wound up in Davy Jones' Locker.

(Several months later in another torpedo attack, two torpedoes had been launched by another Kate and were observed approaching on the starboard bow. Captain Litch ordered flank speed and an emergency turn into the path of the two torpedoes; he delicately steered the ship between them and then wiped the sweat off his brow.)

But our jubilation at noon was to turn to consternation at midnight.

All afternoon we were being shadowed by "Bogies" (enemy airplanes) which were keeping their distance, having learned what had happened to the six Kates at noontime. They waited for the stealth of night.

It was a clear night; starlight and moonlight silhouetted our formation. Then the enemy released many bright flares at high altitude, which lit up the night sky to make it appear like full daylight. In contrast to the usual pitch blackness of normal wartime cruising conditions, it made one feel nakedly exposed.

At that time, my Battle Station was in the Gunnery Control Center, an open area in the island structure above the Navigation Bridge, I was monitoring "Bogey" reports coming from CIC (Combat Information Center). Many "Bogeys" were all around and above us. We kept shifting our fire control directors and guns onto the most threatening, closer-in targets. As targets advanced to within range, our 5-inch anti-aircraft battery opened fire with a "BOOM, BOOM, BOOM" that awakened feelings of both excitement and danger.

As the targets got closer, the 40-mm battery opened fire with a sharp "SPLAT, SPLAT, SPLAT," which heightened the trepidation. Further in, the 20-mm battery opened up with a frantic "RAT, TAT, TAT" and it was time to hold one's breath and say a few prayers.

For some time we went through a number of these firing sequences and we were fortunate to escape damage; the feelings of danger eased as time wore on. However, eventually there appeared a Kate, armed with a torpedo, undeterred by our firepower. The torpedo hit and exploded with a dull THUD. The deck beneath our feet started shaking from side to side and up and down in a sort of spiral motion like a giant shudder.

"MY GOD, WE ARE HIT!!! We failed to shoot down that Kate!"

There were pangs of remorse that our team failed to protect the other shipmates who were relying on us. There was smoke from the fantail. The ship was going around in circles and we couldn't straighten it out. We were sitting ducks with all those flares glaring down on us. We wondered if Kate's brothers would now come in to finish us off.

What would it be like to have to abandon ship?

Make sure your life jacket is secure.

But wait ...

"This is your Captain speaking ... leave the worrying to me. I got you in here and I'm going to get you out. I'm counting on every man to do his job and I will pull us through."

Good old Felix! Fear and trepidation were dispelled by a determination to do our best and see the thing through! The task group was ordered to circle the *Lexington* in the opposite direction to protect her from further attack.

The torpedo had sheared off the outboard starboard propeller, jammed the inboard propeller shaft and had incapacitated the steering gear, locking the rudder at 30 degrees left. That was why we were going around in a circle and couldn't straighten out. Through the sound-powered (voice-powered) telephone system, the crew stationed in the steering gear compartment reported the extent of the damage. The only hope of straightening the rudder was a small, manually-operated hydraulic pump that had been installed by a prescient engineering officer as an alternative for just such an emergency.

Meanwhile, the compartment above the steering gear compartment was flooding and the compartment atmosphere was being poisoned with escaping Freon gas. Breathing was very difficult and the crew requested permission to abandon their station.

The Captain said that he would leave the decision up to the crew, trusting their judgment between duty and personal safety. But he said he wanted them to report to him first if they decided to abandon their station. The crew decided in favor of duty and remained on station long enough to complete their mission; they were then rescued and rushed to sick bay.

Captain Edward Steichen, who was onboard on a photography mission, later remarked to Captain Stump what a wonderful act of trust and leadership it was for him to leave the decision to the crew. He asked what Stump would have done if the crew had decided otherwise. The reply was, "Then I would have had no choice but to order them to stay."

After the war Captain Steichen published his wonderful photographs in a book entitled 'The Blue Ghost" and wrote a moving minute-by-minute account of events leading up to the torpedo hit. It is a book I highly recommend.

With only one starboard propeller and two port propellers operative, the ship could only maintain a speed of 20 knots straight ahead; steering was carefully achieved by regulating the speed of the outboard port propeller.

We were fortunate. It took only a half-hour to straighten out the rudder. It was a relief to get out of that uncontrollable turn. But the sporadic attacks continued and we were fortunate that the ship's electrical power was undiminished. We could continue to track targets and fire our guns to ward off their attacks. As we headed eastward away from the canopy of flares and Bogies, the rest of the Task Force trailed behind us on the horizon, taking the brunt of the attacks.

Finally, at 1:27 a.m., the moon set and, to quote the Quartermaster's log, "Thank God!" The enemy planes retired and our radars indicated all clear.

Our hull had a gaping hole on the starboard side aft at the location of the CPO quarters. We had two crewmen dead, seven missing, thirty-five wounded. Many of our airplanes were damaged by the shock and tremors of the torpedo hit, some so badly that we had to deep-six them.

"17 Zeros to 0" – pilots of Fighting Squadron 16 engaged 21 enemy "Zeros" and splashed 17. All of our F6Fs returned safely.

Burial at sea – Farewell to comrades killed in torpedo hit.

35

We buried our dead at sea in a funeral ceremony. The Captain read the funeral service. The Marine guard fired a volley. The bugler blew "Taps."

Tokyo Rose would announce that their planes had sunk the Blue Ghost, the new *Lexington*. Her report reverberated across the country and the rumors reached the ears of all the families whose sons were stationed aboard the *Lexington*.

Back home, my father was aware of these reports and rumors that seemed to confirm the truth of Tokyo Rose's announcements. But my mother stubbornly refused to accept the reports. "Otto will be home for Christmas." My father thought she was losing her mind. But Mom's faith did not desert her.

In five days we arrived at Pearl Harbor and Lady Lex went into drydock for emergency repairs, including covering a 50-foot hole in her starboard quarter. A week later, on the afternoon of December 17th, we put out to sea and headed for our home port, Bremerton, Washington arriving on December 22nd. At the railroad station in Seattle, trains were waiting for those of us who had been given leave to travel home to our families in time for Christmas.

I arrived in Brooklyn, New York on the 26th of December, only one day late.

CHAPTER 7

WHO'S GOT THE CONN ?

To "conn" a ship is to direct its course and speed and to control other events that take place on the ship. The term "conn" is derived from the "conning tower" (also called the bridge), the commanding officer's station when the ship is underway, from which he controlled the ship's movements and conditions.

In modern practice, the captain selects some junior officers to perform this command function for him during routine cruising conditions or in port. These officers are designated "Officers of the Deck" (OOD's). They perform duties similar to command duty officers in other military services. They stand watches four hours at a time carrying out the captain's orders. The OOD is said to have the "Conn."

While my primary responsibility was to the 8th Division (Fire Control), I was also assigned collateral duties as one of three regular OOD's. My regular duties in the 8th Division were performed when not on watch as OOD.

One of the principal routine duties of the OOD is station-keeping, defined as maintaining the ship's assigned position in the task group formation. The course and speed for the task group is ordered by its Commander, usually a Rear Admiral. The TG commander also designates a guide ship, usually one of the carriers, and all other ships then must keep station on the guide by modifying their course and speed accordingly.

Each ship is assigned a station (relative position) in the formation. A typical task group formation is shown in the accompanying chart. It is defined in polar coordinates (circular and radial dimensions). The aircraft carriers are placed in the inner ring with a radius of 1500 yards (3000 yards diameter). Battleships and cruisers are placed in the intermediate ring with a radius of 3000 yards (6000 yards diameter); these ships provide fire power against enemy planes trying to bomb or torpedo the carriers. The outer ring with a radius of 7000 yards (14,000 yards diameter/or approximately 8 miles), positions the destroyers for defense against enemy submarines.

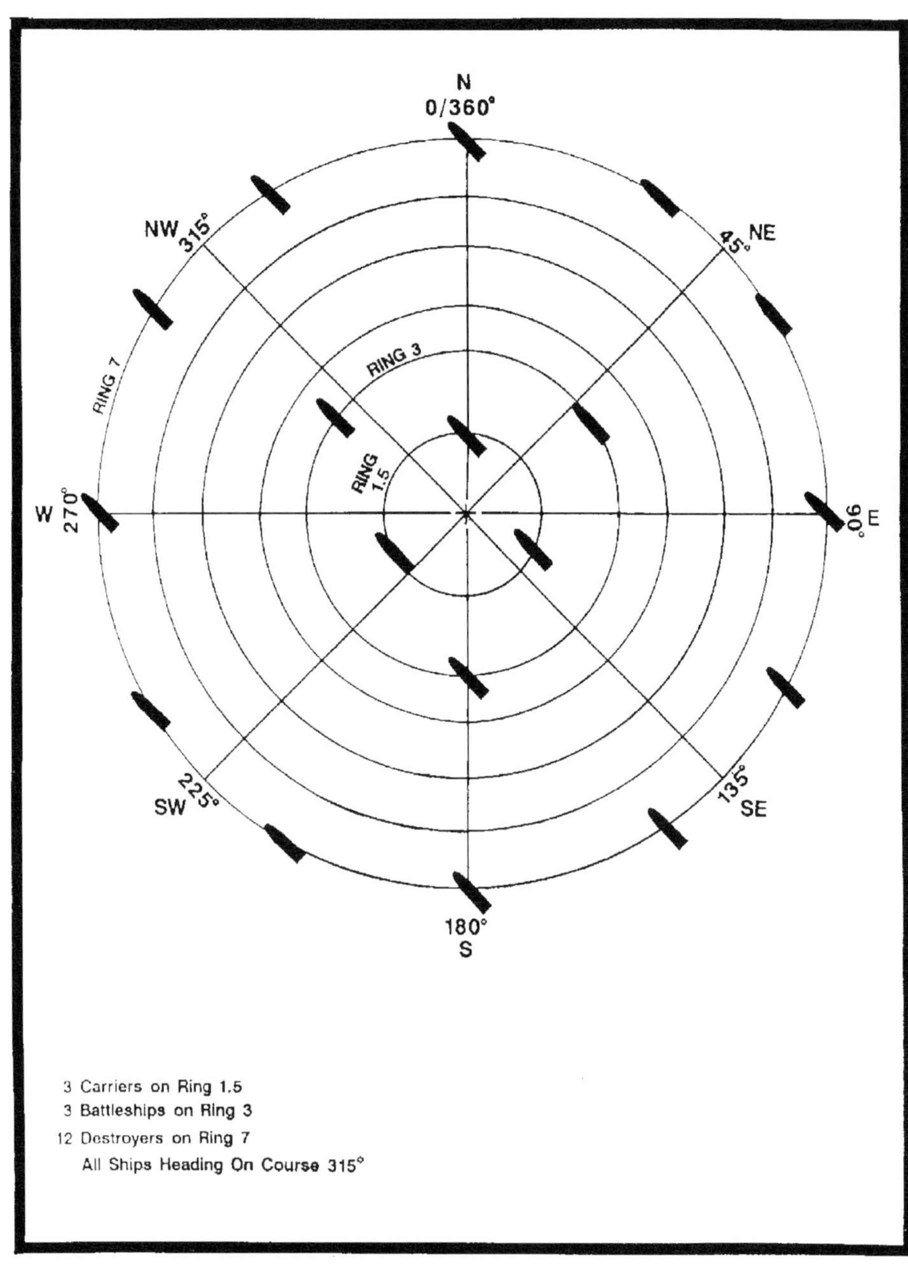

Typical task group formation showing outer screen of destroyers, intermediate ring of anti-aircraft support ships (battleships or cruisers) around inner core or aircraft carriers.

The advantage of the circular formation was that all ships could maneuver and change course simultaneously. The traditional battleship line of battle had to change course in succession.

In addition to their primary mission of protecting the carriers, the battleships and cruisers conduct shore bombardment for landing operations; also in the event of a surface engagement with enemy surface units, they pull out of the task group formation and maneuver in traditional line of battle while the carriers withdraw from the immediate scene of the surface engagement and attack the enemy with bombs and torpedoes. (While this scenario was never fully orchestrated, it was avoided during the Leyte Gulf battle when Admiral "Bull" Halsey pulled away from guarding the San Bernadino Straits to pursue a decoy force abreast of Northern Luzon).

Another advantage of the circular formation was that it permitted one carrier to perform flight operations independently, within the confines of the destroyer ring (8 miles in diameter) while the task group could continue steaming on a course which permitted making necessary headway to a designated position. (See Flight Operations).

The mid-watch routine started with a wake-up call by a messenger at 2330 (11:30 p.m.). You usually had been asleep for only an hour when the call came. The first thing you had to do was to put on your red plastic glasses in order to establish your sensitivity to the darkness. Then you had a cup of hot black coffee in the wardroom to wake you up out of your zombie-like state. The coffee had been brewed at 0500 that morning and was reputed to be so strong that the spoon floated on the surface.

Then you went out on deck through a vestibule arrangement so that no light escaped from the interior to provide a target for an enemy submarine. The bridge was illuminated with very dim red lights on dials such as the compass heading and the local zone time. You read the captain's night orders such as base course heading and zigzag pattern number and relieved the 2000-2400 OOD.

Your first concern was your station in the formation, your heading for the proper time sequence in the zigzag plan and the next leg of the course change. Zigzag course changes occurred at odd times and at odd amounts and you had to be ready with your order to the helmsman and visually verify his compliance.

On a quiet night I would occasionally relieve the helmsman at the wheel and have him and the JOOD call out the course changes and check my steering accuracy. Thirty-six thousand tons of steel has a tremendous inertia. There was a lag time of about 30 seconds between the time you put the rudder over and when you detected a slight movement in the course heading. The trick was anticipatory synchronization. It was gratifying to keep the 36,000-ton behemoth on a steady course.

One night we were at anchor at the Eniwetok Atoll and my mid-watch station was at the quarterdeck at the gangway on the port side of the hangar deck. At about 0200 I heard a "swish-swish" sound on the accomodation ladder. I had heard no boat approaching and as I looked down I saw an apparition of a white T-shirt and khaki trousers coming up the ladder. At the top of the ladder I saw a young man drenching wet.

"Who are you?"

"I am Lt. Lodge from the USS *Enterprise*."

"How did you get here?"

"I've been swimming since dusk."

He'd been ashore at the "O" Club and had had a few drinks. While waiting at the dock for the boat from the *Enterprise* to pick him up he got into a fight with a captain. When the shore patrol approached to arrest him, he jumped into the water and started swimming. About seven hours later, thoroughly soaked but also sobered up, he arrived at the *Lexington's* sea ladder.

"So, what can I do for you?"

"I need some coffee, some dry clothes and a lift back to the *Enterprise*."

I got him some coffee, gave him some dry clothing and at dawn, arranged for a boat to take him to his ship. His parting words were, "Thanks for your kindness. When this war is over, come to see me in Boston. My family is influential there."

As a 23-year-old junior officer, the responsibility of the conn of a 36,000-ton aircraft carrier, comprising some 90 aircraft and 3,500 men weighed heavily on me. On a busy morning watch (0800-noon) keeping station in the formation, overseeing flight operations, dealing with unexpected crises, could create a lot of tension.

After one such harrowing watch, I would go into the chart room to write in the log all significant happenings which occurred during the watch. My hands would still be trembling from the tension. Standing in front of the chart table, I would be confronted by a sign put up by the Quartermaster. **"CHEER UP"** it said in large-size type. Immediately below it in small type it said, "the worst is yet to come." The dark humor drained the tension from my body. I could then go down to the wardroom and enjoy my lunch.

(See copy of typical log entry.) The ship's Organization Book specified that under special conditions, such as flight operations or when coming into port, a senior officer must take the conn. Under those circumstances, when the Navigator or the Captain takes the conn, the OOD assists with a plotting board or provides some other function.

0800-01200 Steaming as before. 0800 Made daily inspection of all magazines and smokeless powder samples. Condition normal. Mustered crew on stations. No absentees. Rendezvoused with Task Unit 30.1.7, commenced fuel exercises. Formed fueling disposition 5-Roger (modified), axis 070^{0}(T), fueling course 070^{0}(T), fueling speed 10 knots (075 RPM). Tankers normal to course, left to right at 1500 yard intervals, Neches, Atascosa (guide 3-350), Taluga and Niobrara. Made all preparation to fuel from tanker. 0803 Changed fleet course to 085^{0}(T). Maneuvering independently on various courses and speeds to go alongside AO Neches. 0845 Enterprise, Independence plus escorting destroyers rejoined formation and assumed previously assigned stations. 0849 Towline secured to Neches. 0900 Commenced taking aboard fuel oil and aviation gasoline, completing at 1102, having received 78,000 gallons of aviation gasoline and 239,732 gallons of fuel oil at 60^{0}F. 0904 Received DD Miller alongside for transfer of personnel. Pursuant to orders of the Commanding Officer, authority, Chief of Naval Personnel dispatch dated December 11, 1944, Lt. Comdr R.G. Allen (A), USNR was detached. 0920 Cast off DD Miller, having transferred 7 pilots to ferry replacement aircraft. 0925 Received Stephen Potter alongside port quarter, cast off at 0927, after delivery of Officer Messenger Mail. 0943 Let fires die out under boiler No. 4. 0945 By order of the Commanding Officer, Fournier, T.J., Slc, USNR, was released from confinement and restored to duty, the period of confinement imposed on him by summary court martial having expired. 1005 Jettisoned F6F No. 43, Bureau No. 71563. 1006 Cut out boiler No. 4 from the main steam line. 1015 Received DD Sperry alongside for transfer of Lt. R.E. McHenry (Al), USNR, Butler, C.T. ARM3c, 824 97 55, USNR, and Fletcher, C.D., AMM2c, 312 25 19, USN, who made water landing on Jan. 6 inside of formation. 1030 Received DD Hanks alongside for transfer of aviation stores, cast off at 1042. 1049 Received DD Trathen alongside for transfer of Million, W.R., MM2c, 615 56 63, USNR requiring medical attention, cast off at 1052. 1109 Castoff AO Neches, hauled clear of tanker, commenced maneuvering independently to regain station in formation. 1120 Jettisoned F6F(N) No. 50, Bureau No. 58553 damaged beyond repair.

Sample log entry for one four-hour watch.

As an OOD I had assisted the Navigator and Captain in this manner frequently and gained the confidence of the Captain because of my ability to conn the ship during flight operations. When a new Navigator came aboard, a full Commander, for some reason our Captain did not develop the same confidence in him.

On one occasion, preparing for flight operations, the new Navigator came on the bridge to relieve me. He ordered a change in course and speed but Captain Litch stuck his head around the wing of the bridge and counter-manded the new orders with a "Belay that!", signifying he was taking the conn. Almost immediately after that he turned to me and said, "Rummy, take the conn."

It was an unprecedented action. The poor Navigator was flabbergasted, crushed. I felt badly for him. But later I felt proud that the Captain had more confidence in me than in him.

To commemorate the incident, my JOOD, Ensign Kalina drew a cartoon entitled "Who's Got The Conn?".

The following year Captain Litch was, in normal rotation, succeeded by Captain Robbins. At the time, I never received any indication that Robbins shared Litch's confidence in my ability. But many years later, reviewing the contents of my "jacket" (personnel file), I read Captain Robbin's entry in my fitness report: "Qualified by experience to conn a capital ship during war time in the war zone." To me that is the highest accolade a junior naval officer can receive. My proudest memory.

But there was another proud moment, experienced on the spot! Sometime in the fall of 1944 we were anchored in Ulithi Atoll, our forward base for repairs, replenishment and resting. I had the mid-watch (midnight to 0400) as OOD. Since we were at anchor, my station was at the quarterdeck on the port side of the hangar deck. When I took the conn at midnight, there were four boats tied to the stern, but there were only three boats at 03:45 when my relief showed up. The most likely scenario was that the line holding one of the motor whaleboats had loosened and the boat had drifted away.

Although the coxswain who had last used the boat had not secured the line properly, I was responsible for losing the boat because it had broken loose during my watch. I had a vision of being court-martialed and disgraced. I had to find that boat.

I went up to the chart room to check positions of other ships anchored in the atoll. I checked the direction of the wind and tide and decided the boat would have drifted in a westerly direction. I then estimated how far the boat could have drifted in 2 to 3 hours and checked to see which ships were anchored to the west of us.

I rustled up a crew for the other motor whaleboat and set out at about 0400 in the pitch darkness. There were lights on the accommodation ladders of the ships anchored along the westerly direction I had estimated and I hailed the duty officer of each ship and asked if he had seen our boat. No luck. I eventually ran out of ships in the direction I was heading.

I decided to continue westward and if I didn't see the boat along the way I would then overshoot the position.

I had estimated the distance the boat had drifted in the past 3 to 4 hours. I kept looking left and right and occasionally, backward but it was still too dark to see anything more than 30 or 40 yards away.

The faint light of dawn started to emerge behind us and it confirmed that we had not strayed from our course. As the eastern sky got brighter, I spotted a small dark object floating about 2,000 yards away. "Turn around!" The closer we got the more we became certain it was our boat.

I told the coxswain and the engineer to man the lost boat. I assigned the lineman to operate the engine of our boat and I took the tiller.

What a relief! No court-martial! What a wonderful feeling, what a joyful exuberance I experienced. I felt like Columbus sighting land in the West Indies in 1492. All we had to do was follow the sun - and we got back to the ship about 0730 and tied the two boats to the fantail.

I told my relief, who still had the conn, that four boats were now his responsibility. Then I went to breakfast to satisfy a ravenous appetite, just in time for morning quarters and the start of a new day.

We had a radar repeater on the bridge which was indispensable for station-keeping, particularly at night; it provided accurate range and bearing to the guide. One night, on the mid-watch, I spent an anxious two to three hours with my eyes glued to the screen.

A new carrier had joined the task group and to make its job easier, the admiral decided to designate it as the task group guide. The group was ordered to zig-zag according to a specified plan. Soon after midnight, I noticed that my range and bearing to the guide kept changing, requiring constant adjustment in course and speed to regain position. I was wondering what was going on.

The zig-zag plan required changes every few minutes to a new course. The changes had to be made precisely on the minute so that all ships would change synchronistically. I made sure we were using the specified plan number.

Watching the screen, I noticed that other ships in the formation were also getting out of position; it was not our fault alone, it appeared to be only the guide that was getting out of position. But of course the guide cannot get out of position; all other ships must follow the guide.

I received an intra-ship phone call from the flag duty officer, "What is happening with the guide?" I replied that all other ships were straying off station. He sent a TBS radio message to the guide "POSIT," meaning, take your station in the formation. But of course this order was confusing and was apparently understood to follow the flagship, designating the *Lexington* as the guide. But this misinterpretation now led to another problem.

It soon became apparent that the guide's radar range did not match the *Lexington's* radar range. I kept adjusting my course to open the range to the guide; he kept adjusting his course to close the distance between us. As a consequence, the whole formation kept drifting off course. I didn't know what to do; doctrine did not permit me to radio the guide directly.

The confusion lasted until about 0330, when I surmised that the guide's relieving OOD had reviewed the situation and taken control. I wiped my brow and breathed a sigh of relief.

<u>*CHAPTER 8*</u>

FLIGHT OPERATIONS

Flight operations were the most hectic day-to-day operations on an aircraft carrier. Of course the launching and retrieval of aircraft were the critical operations, requiring the skills of pilots and Control personnel. But the greatest number of personnel involved plane handlers, who moved planes in place around the flight deck for speedy launching, up and down massive elevators between the flight deck and hangar deck. A gang of mechanics kept the planes in tip-top condition and a host of ammunition handlers brought up bombs, missiles and torpedoes topside on ammunition hoists and loaded the planes.

All of these activities were the responsibility of the Air Officer. As part of ships company, my concern was to provide suitable flying conditions such as relative wind speed and direction.

There were two ways that we conducted flight operations. The first was that the whole task group would adopt the course and speed determined by the carrier which is launching or recovering aircraft. The whole task group would move as a unit. This procedure also applied when more than one carrier was conducting flight operations simultaneously.

The other procedure involved the carrier maneuvering independently within the confines of the destroyer screen, while the task group continued on a course and speed mandated by tactical considerations.

For either method of operations, the first step in plotting the ship's course for flight operations was to measure the direction and speed of the wind in order to get maximum wind speed across the deck. Wind speed across the deck (also known as relative wind) is a combination of true wind speed and ship speed. The "Air Boss" would specify the minimum speed needed. A loaded TBF (torpedo plane) required a minimum of approximately 120 mph of wind over its wings to become airborne. This total "wind over wing" speed could be made up of wind speed across the deck plus airplane speed over the deck (derived from the plane's propeller or ship's catapult). A typical combination would be:

True wind speed (TWS)	10 knots
Ship speed	20 knots
Plane speed across deck	90 knots
Total:	120 knots

True wind speed and direction would normally vary constantly. If TWS was low, the OOD would call for higher ship speed. Maximum ship speed for the *Lexington* was in excess of 30 knots.

Also, with low true wind speed, true wind direction would normally not be steady so the OOD or conning officer had to "chase the wind" because relative wind direction had to be five degrees on the port bow. This was critical particularly when landing aircraft, to avoid air turbulence in the landing zone abaft the island structure.

The OOD, and the Air Boss, would nervously watch the indicator of relative wind speed and direction. When satisfied, the Air Boss would order "Launch Planes."

The second method of operation (carrier moving independently of task group) requires the use of a maneuvering board (see chart) and graphical plot:

First draw vectors of task group course and speed and own ship course and speed to determine relative movement course and speed vector between own ship and task group. In the example, the task group must proceed on course 315 at 18 knots while own ship must steer on course 005 degrees at 20 knots into a 10-knot wind coming from the north.

From those two vectors, the relative movement vector is graphically measured to be 16 knots and, with the use of a set of parallel rulers, in the direction of 064 degrees. This direction is the desired direction of traverse through the formation. With the set of parallel rulers, a clear line of traverse (track) between different ships in the formation is selected.

There are a number of different lines of traverse that would entail a satisfactory solution. The line drawn on the chart passes between the battleship at 180 degrees Ring 3 and the carrier at 120 degrees Ring 1.5.

It gives sufficient leeway passing ahead of the battleship but a little less passing behind the carrier.

The starting point for this line of traverse would be in the southwest quadrant, close to the destroyer ring. The termination point would be in the northeast quadrant; if flight operations are not completed before the carrier reaches the destroyer ring the destroyer is requested to accompany own ship outside the destroyer ring until the last plane is landed.

Upon completion of flight operations, the conning officer may want to increase the ship's speed in order to resume his assigned station in the formation as quickly as possible.

This maneuver is the fun part of the conning officer's job.

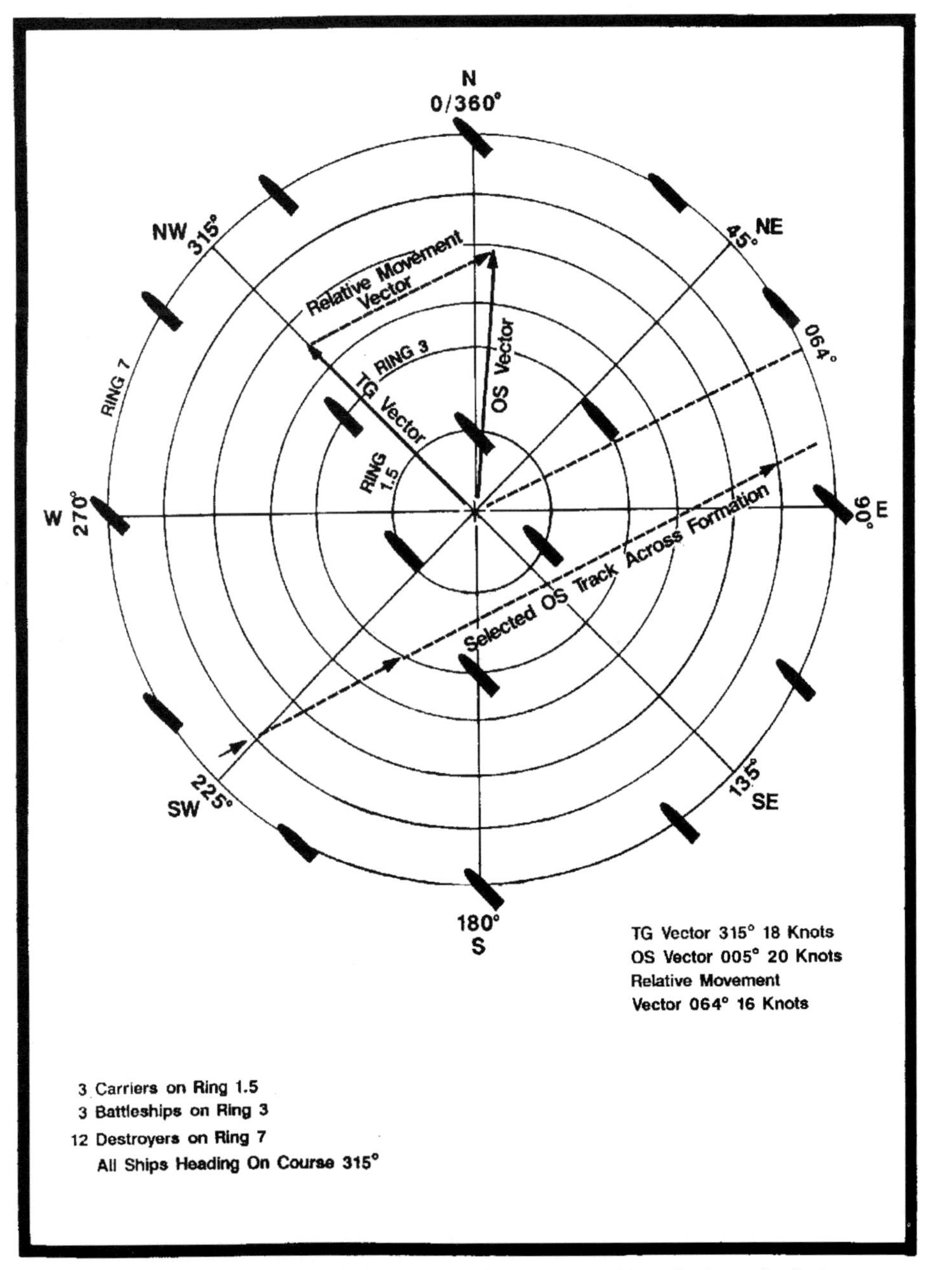

Maneuvering inside formation showing graphic solution of relative movement of single carrier conducting flight operations.

CHAPTER 9

COLLISION

EASTER MORN 1944

The *Lexington* had a temperamental steering engine which used hydraulic power to move the massive rudder and hold it in position when changing the heading of the 36,000 ton ship.

The engine had the habit of occasionally and without warning losing control of the rudder during a turn.

This peculiarity was the bane of every OOD who had to respond immediately by blowing four blasts on the ship's horn to warn adjacent ships and then inform them by short-range TBS radio about the direction in which his turn was uncontrollable. The nightmare was the possibility of a collision with another 36,000 ton carrier or battleship in the formation.

Credit the alertness of the OOD and OOD's in accompanying ships in avoiding a collision in this situation. But the collision described below occurred when the *Lexington* was tied to a pier in a shipyard.

The USS *Lexington* was tied to a pier in the Bremerton shipyard, a 50-minute ferry trip from Seattle, in the final stages of repairing torpedo damage sustained in the Kwajalein strike three months earlier. Half of the ship's crew was on leave, a quarter was ashore on liberty, and I was in the quarter of the group that had the duty. I had the morning watch as OOD. The Senior Officer on board was Lt.Cdr. Cecil Dowling, a pre-war Chief Warrant Boatswain.

Everything was peaceful and quiet except for the snoring of the yard workmen and the ship was in good hands with me on the quarterdeck. The hour was approximately 0530. Dawn was just breaking and I was watching another Essex-class carrier, the USS *Ticonderoga*, being pulled out of dry dock from the head of our pier, offset from it.

There was a brisk wind blowing from the East which caught the *Ticonderoga* as she cleared the shelter of the 4-story industrial building alongside the eastern side of the dry dock. Three tugs were pulling the carrier past the *Lexington* out to the stream where she could maneuver under her own power. But the wind was too strong and she started slipping sideways toward the *Lexington*.

My first impulse was to ring the engine room for emergency power but of course, the power plant was shut down and the "Black Gang" (the engineering crew) was asleep. Then, as the *Ticonderoga* continued to drift toward us and it was obvious that a collision was imminent, I realized the only thing I could do was to ring the General Alarm for Collision Quarters.

The sound of the GQ alarm bells, not heard for several months during battle conditions, made my blood freeze and gave me a sick feeling in the pit of my stomach. I can still picture old Cecil hobbling down the hangar deck in slippers and a bathrobe and puffing "What's happening Rummy?" (short for Romanelli, no allusion to my drinking habits).

The *Ticonderoga* scraped our starboard side from midships to stern, wiping out one sponson (a gun platform projecting from the side of the ship), several radio antennas and started several small fires which were quickly extinguished by our damage control skeleton crew on station. There was only superficial damage, which was easily repairable. "Well done Rummy!" said Cecil as he shuffled back to his stateroom. Of course, all I did, or could do was to ring the alarm. As far as I am aware, this was the only time in Naval history that an OOD involved in a collision received a commendation.

The collision could not have happened at a more opportune time or place for immediate repairs.

<u>*CHAPTER 10*</u>

TYPHOONS

THE OTHER ENEMY

In the novel and in the motion picture, "The Caine Mutiny," the crew of the USS *Caine* wrested control of the ship from Captain Queeg (played by Humphrey Bogart) during a typhoon in the Pacific.

Queeg's fear of the fury of the storm preyed on his paranoia which led to his helpless inactivity, leaving him unable to take measures to survive the storm. Mutiny is a very serious event in the U.S. Navy, punishable by death if not determined to be justifiable. Tradition has it that there has never been a mutiny in the U.S. Navy.

Bogart's performance expertly reflects the script but the film's use of artistic license to achieve dramatic impact, portrays character elements that I have never observed in a naval officer.

I strongly feel this characterization was extremely unfair to all the senior naval officers with whom I have been acquainted either personally or by reputation. Among these I list Captains Felix Stump and Ernest Litch and Admirals Marc Mitscher, Raymond Spruance and Chester Nimitz, whose competence, courage, compassion, dedication, integrity and leadership I admired.

And I particularly admired the thousands of young pilots, most of whom were even younger than myself, for their exuberance and fearlessness in pursuing the enemy, even in the face of the high rates of attrition in flying off aircraft carriers at sea (the "operational casualties").

For their sacrilege, I would sentence the author and screenwriter of "The Caine Mutiny" to cross the Pacific Ocean during typhoon season in a leaky rowboat, along with Humphrey Bogart, for his indiscretion and defamation of character.

However, the "Caine" script deals with a dilemma that is not uncommon in military operations – the conflict between authority and the exigencies of particular situations – a dilemma it shares with the Third Fleet experience in one typhoon.

Following are three accounts of the ravages of typhoons on naval vessels. The first situation demonstrates Captain Stump's high standards of performance in a difficult fueling-at-sea situation. The second situation deals with the dilemma mentioned above. The third situation describes briefly the damage a furious typhoon can inflict on steel warships.

During the fall of 1943, the task force was enroute to a target in the Marshall Islands when a typhoon was reported in its path. At the forward edge of the typhoon, the fleet was engaged in a fueling-at-sea operation preparatory to the upcoming engagement. Fueling at sea was normally a dangerous operation. With the two ships running side by side, the current between the two ships was a raceway. The Bernoulli effect of the underwater shapes of the two ships hulls tended to draw the ships together with a high risk of collision.

The high winds and rough seas were seriously disrupting the progress of fueling by snapping fueling lines and hawsers between the *Lexington* and the tanker. Lt. Cmdr. Cecil Dowling, the Fueling Officer, was acknowledged to be the fleet's most capable officer for fueling at sea,but nature would not be denied.

Captain Stump was on the starboard wing of the bridge keeping a sharp eye on the progress of fueling. He became increasingly impatient with the delays occasioned by disruption of hawsers and fuel hoses. The Captain was a perfectionist.

When fueling was finally completed, about an hour longer than the usual one and one-half hours, the Captain had the word passed on the ship's loudspeaker. "Now – the Engineering Officer and the First Lieutenant report to the bridge on the double!" Ordering two senior officers to report "on the double" (run all the way) was considered a slap in the face and the entire ship knew it. The "First Lieutenant" was actually a Commander who was responsible for the ship's structural integrity including repairs, fire fighting, damage control, flooding, fueling and arranging ballast.

In the Captain's sea cabin, just aft of the bridge, the Captain commenced his harangue at the weary and cowed Engineering Officer and First Lieutenant. "Never in all my years at sea have I ever seen such unseamanlike inefficiency and sloppy action ..." The harangue had continued for about 15 minutes when there was a knock on the cabin door.

The Marine orderly handed the Captain a radio message from Admiral Sherman. Felix quickly and silently read the message and expressed a bemused, "Humph!". Then he turned and addressed his two senior offic-

Fueling at sea – showing the froth between carrier and tanker running side-by-side in a relatively calm sea.

ers. "Let me read you what Admiral Sherman has to say, 'Congratulations. *Lexington* was the only ship to complete fueling operations. Well Done!'

There, you see, the Admiral does not know his ass from a hot rock. Gentlemen, you are dismissed."

On December 17, 1944, the Third Fleet under Admiral Halsey rendezvoused with their oilers 500 miles east of Luzon, preparatory to a strike on that island. But fueling at sea could not be completed because a major typhoon was building up. This typhoon, with winds of 93 knots and waves 75 feet trough to crest, was one of the worst in decades.

From the bridge of the *Lexington* it appeared as if the bow would plow into the trough of an oncoming wave and continue straight down. As the bow plowed into an oncoming wave, the stern rose out of the water and the ship's propellers churned air instead of water.

With a lever arm of about 600 feet from its center of gravity, the ship's bow was going up and down like an express elevator. Walking forward to my stateroom, located just aft of the chain locker in the forecastle, my knees would buckle when the bow rose on a wave and my feet would churn air when the bow headed down into the trough. Waves breaking over the flight deck tore airplanes from their moorings and swept them into the sea.

An aircraft carrier has a high freeboard and a flight deck that overhangs the hull. In high winds it acts like a sail and sluggishly refuses to respond to its rudder. On occasion, it would require the torque action of the port and starboard propellers turning in opposition in order to effect a turn to a new course.

At the start of the fueling operation the destroyers were scheduled to be fueled after the capital ships (carriers, battleships, cruisers). They were ordered to be ready to fuel within 10 minutes notice. This meant that perhaps an hour ahead of time they had to empty ballast tanks to receive fuel. In the meantime they were riding high in the water, not very stable in rough weather.

As the intensity of the storm increased and all fueling operations were discontinued, the order to be ready to fuel within 10 minutes was not rescinded and the destroyers, with their high buoyancy were bobbing like corks on angry waves, in danger of capsizing. The destroyer captains were caught in a dilemma: obey standing orders or take on ballast in the empty tanks to restore stability to their ships. The Fleet Admiral, "Bull" Halsey was apparently not aware of this dilemma and so let stand the previous order; apparently he was oblivious to the life-and-death danger to the destroyers in his fleet.

USS Bennington – victim of typhoon. Steel support beams collapsed as the ship's bow and forward flight deck plowed into 80-foot waves. Repairs were made at a forward base.

Many of the destroyer captains chose to disobey the ready-to-fuel order and thus saved their ships. Of those destroyers whose captains chose to follow the Admiral's standing order, or decided too late to ignore it, three destroyers capsized and sank, taking the lives of 800 men. One destroyer recorded a roll of 74 degrees but did not sink.

A Court of Inquiry determined that Admiral Halsey was primarily responsible for these losses, despite the contradictory weather reports.

Because of storm damage to carriers and loss of aircraft, the Luzon strike was cancelled. The fleet returned to Ulithi for repairs and replenishment.

As severe as the typhoon of December, 1944 was, the typhoon of June, 1945 off the island of Okinawa was worse. The *Lexington* had just arrived from Bremerton after a badly needed overhaul. On two Essex-class carriers, the *Bennington* and the *Hornet*, their forward flight decks collapsed. On the heavy cruiser *Pittsburgh*, 100 feet of her bow was torn off. Fortunately, no destroyers were sunk.

In these two typhoons, the Japanese must have invoked the fury of their "divine wind" as the last word in a defense that was failing them in almost every other way.

CHAPTER 11

TURKEY SHOOT

By the spring of 1944, the "Fast Carrier Task Force" had grown to 15 of the new "Fast Carriers" with support ships of seven "Fast Battleships" and additional cruisers, destroyers, fueling tankers and other logistics support vessels.

Recognizing the superiority of these forces, the Joint Chiefs of Staff decided to leapfrog over the island-by-island strategy and take a strong position in the Marianas Island of Saipan. A strong position there, so much closer to the Japanese islands, could control shipping and air access to many more island bases and essentially cause them to "die on the vine," without wasting time and the lives of our sailors, Marines and soldiers on the island-by-island recovery strategy.

It was recognized that our thrust at the Saipan strategic location would result in a strong retaliation by the Japanese fleet and so the Fifth Fleet, with Admiral Raymond Spruance, was assigned to protect our landing forces against the Japanese fleet and land-based aircraft attacks from surrounding Japanese-held islands.

The battle which ensued has been called "The First Battle of the Philippine Sea" and also "The Greatest Carrier-to-Carrier Battle" by some historians because of the great number of aircraft involved and also because no significant surface forces were involved. The Fifth Fleet had 15 "Fast Carriers"; the Japanese fleet had 9.

However, the battle was named "The Marianas Turkey Shoot" by our pilots because of the overwhelming one-sided destruction of the attacking Japanese fleet aircraft. Over 465 aircraft were destroyed, the core of experienced carrier-based pilots. This loss crippled the future of Japanese air-strike capability. None of our carriers were damaged.

Prior to landing the Army and Marine invasion troops, the Fifth Fleet undertook softening operations with air strikes and shore bombardment at airports and military shore facilities to "sweep the area clean" of any Japanese forces that might threaten our invasion forces.

Admiral Chester Nimitz, commander of all Naval forces in the Pacific Ocean.

Admiral Raymond Spruance, commander of the Fifth Fleet at Marianas Turkey Shoot and during the defense of Midway.

Vice Admiral Marc Mitscher, commander of the Fast Carrier Task Force.

An additional 370 land-based enemy aircraft were destroyed during the battle.

When the landing started, the Fifth Fleet provided close-support actions to assist our ground forces. The Japanese defenders provided fierce resistance to our Marine and Army troops.

Admiral Spruance arranged Task Force 58 task groups in a line north and south to the west of Saipan to allow each task group to conduct flight operations independently into an easterly wind. Battleships and cruisers were formed in Task Force Group 54 and positioned to the west of the line of carrier groups to provide early anti-aircraft fire power from the expected approach of enemy strikes. *Lexington* was assigned to Task Group 58.3 and carried Adm. Mitscher's flag.

Spruance received intelligence reports when the main groups of the Japanese fleet sortied from their bases and also received enroute reports, so he was expecting them to arrive into the battle area around June 20th.

Excitement was running high all through Task Force, at the prospect of the coming battle. The pilots, in particular, were eager to attack the warships and test the mettle of their Grumman F6F fighters against the Japanese Zeros. They couldn't wait for Spruance to rush out west to engage the enemy fleet as soon as possible.

But Spruance, known as the Navy's most brilliant tactician, held his forces in protective position close to Saipan. That was his primary mission, so he held his fire. Furthermore, he had not received a recent sighting of the enemy fleet's location. A couple of days later, in early morning, our powerful surface radars detected large groups of bogeys (enemy aircraft) stacked in different elevations from sea-level to 20,000 feet altitude, distant 150 miles. This was it! Send out our fighter-interceptors in massive force.

Our fighters caught the Japanese dive bombers, torpedo bombers and Zeros by surprise. It was a slaughter. Most of the Japanese planes that escaped our F6Fs were shot down by surface ship anti-aircraft guns, including a squadron of enemy torpedo planes trying to filter through Task Force 54's seven Fast Battleships. None got through. By mid-afternoon the count was over 400 enemy planes.

The enemy had launched their attack from a distance of 500 miles. Their strategy was to attack the Fifth Fleet and invasion ships, then land at airfields on Saipan. After refueling and rearming their planes would start back, attack the invasion forces and Fifth Fleet a second time, then head back west to their home carriers.

It was a strategy of wishful thinking that fell apart when 90 percent of their planes were shot down by Fifth Fleet's F6Fs and AA batteries and the remaining 10 percent could not find friendly airfields in Saipan.

By mid-afternoon Spruance received a sighting report of the location of the enemy fleet and it became obvious (by the count of downed enemy planes) that the Japanese forces had "shot their load." By joint agreement between Admiral Spruance and Admiral Mitscher, it was decided to "go get the surface ships," Of course our pilots cheered.

It was recognized that the Japanese fleet was located at a distance close to the maximum range of our attacking aircraft and that our planes would be returning during darkness; but with the threat to our landing forces now eliminated, we could no longer postpone the opportunity of an offensive.

Our strike found the enemy fleet at dusk and immediately started bombing runs. Our planes sank one first-line carrier and two oilers and shot down 65 carrier planes. Another first-line carrier was severely damaged and three escort carriers slightly damaged.

Having expended all their bombs and torpedoes in the fading light, our planes started straggling back to their carriers in small groups, cutting back on their throttles to conserve gas. The carriers had started steaming west at 22 knots to shorten the return distance for the aircraft. But there was also the additional problem of finding their home carriers in absolute darkness, provided their fuel lasted long enough. Very few of the pilots had experienced landing at night.

Contemplating the desperate plight of the returning pilots, those of us on the carriers felt a lump in our throats. This included Admiral Mitscher, who had ordered that the strike take place in late afternoon, knowing that the return would be in total darkness. His compassion elicited a startling order to all carriers:

"Turn on the lights!!!"

He had made a painful decision in ordering his beloved pilots to fly off at maximum distance and return in unaccustomed blackness; that was his duty. Now, listening to radio reports of planes lost and ditching into the sea, his heart spoke:

"Turn on the lights!!!"

And the rest of us on board ship felt the tightness in our throats relax. We were doing the only thing that could be done to lead our "kid brothers" home, at the risk of exposing our ships to any submarines or bombers in the area.

Fortunately, we encountered no enemy submarines and the two enemy planes that tried to land on our carriers were given wave-offs.

"ODE TO LEXINGTON"

The night was dark
The flight was long
The fuel was migthy low
The seas had claimed so many lives
With many more to go.
Oh Lexington, Oh Lexington, please shine your
light for me
And spare my soul, oh once again
From cold and lonely seas .

Up through the clouds
There came a light
A flickering ray of hope
A silent prayer of teared relief
We'd finally made it home.
Oh Lexington, Oh Lexington, arising from the hue
Ole Rose's ghost had come again
To save her flying crew.

– Gregory R. Sawyer, Lt, USN

(Printed on the 45th Anniversary of the USS Lexington.)

But landing operations were extremely chaotic because of crashes, tail hooks not catching and planes landing on "sister" carriers. Radio signals from ditched aircraft were recorded on the charts; that night and in the following days, rescue ships and float planes searched the reported downings. Approximately half of the pilots and crews from the ditched planes were rescued.

After recovering aircraft and conducting search-and-rescue operations, the enemy fleet (what was left of it), had broken off the engagement and was now out of range of our forces. Their losses of more than 465 fleet aircraft and pilots (93%) and three first-line carriers, as compared to 200 aircraft and 50 pilots and crewmen on our side, was a very serious loss. There was no question of our overwhelming victory.

But on our side there was some strong criticism of Admiral Spruance's decision not to attack the enemy fleet earlier, thereby letting the major part of the enemy surface fleet "escape." These critics did not acknowledge that Spruance accomplished: 1) his primary mission of protecting the landing forces (they sustained hardly a scratch) 2) the destruction of 93% of the enemy's fleet aircraft and experienced pilots and 3) the sinking of three first-line carriers without any significant damage to our carriers.

Admiral Mitscher and his chief of staff, "31-knot" Burke had been in favor of attacking earlier. But Spruance's "boss," Admiral Nimitz, did not criticize him, reporting "There is no surmising how a hand might have been played and how much more could have been won ..." Monday morning quarter-backing.

The "hawks" are quick to criticize so-called "missed opportunities." But compare Spruance to the "hawk" commander in the Battle of Leyte Gulf and the consequences of leaving your "sentry post" to chase the "bait." And what about missing further opportunities?

CHAPTER 12

LEYTE GULF

Because of the success of the Marianas Turkey Shoot and raids on other Japanese-held islands close to the Philippine Islands, Admiral Halsey was confident that the U.S. Navy could take a giant step and successfully support General MacArthur's invasion of the Philippines. He made a personal visit to MacArthur to explain his plan and received MacArthur's approval.

When the invasion of Leyte Gulf started, the Japanese Navy high command decided they could not accept the loss of the Philippines. They decided on an all-out effort; they would commit all their principal naval forces in a do-or-die effort to destroy MacArthur's invasion forces in Leyte Gulf.

The Battle for Leyte Gulf (also called the "Second Battle of the Philippine Sea") has been called by Admiral Samuel Eliot Morison, "The greatest naval battle of all time." He devoted the entire Volume XII in his monumental "History of United States Naval Operations in World War II" to this battle. Please refer to that volume for a detailed account of the strategy, tactics, participating forces and key personnel. That battle can also be characterized as the "Swan Song" of the Japanese fleet. The actions ranged over 700 miles North-South in the Philippine Sea and some 400 miles East-West into the Philippine Archipelago.

My purpose is to provide a brief summary of the different forces and battles and highlight the heroic effort of the 7th Fleet "Baby Flattops" and the bravery of the destroyer and destroyer-escort captains who undertook suicide attacks on the Japanese battleships, cruisers and destroyers that were threatening our landing forces at Leyte Gulf.

I also want to draw attention to the great blunder committed by the Third Fleet Commander. Admiral Halsey, which permitted enemy battleships to sink two destroyers, one destroyer escort and two escort carriers; also the missed opportunity to engage in the last battleship-to-battleship engagement in naval history. (Our battleships, Task Group 34, would have had the additional advantage of Task Force 38's tremendous air power.)

The U.S. forces in the battle consisted of the Seventh Fleet, commanded by General Douglas MacArthur, and thereby dubbed "MacArthur's Navy."

MacArthur's subordinate commander for Navy units was Admiral Kincaid. The fleet was composed of U.S. Army troops in landing ships and naval protective forces including six old battleships that had been raised from their graves in Pearl Harbor and repaired. There were also 18 escort carriers in three groups, code-named Taffy One, Two and Three, commanded by Admirals T.L Sprague, Felix Stump (formerly captain of the *Lexington*) and C.A.F. Sprague (no relation to T.L.). The escort carrier airplanes, approximately 30 for each carrier, provided cover for the landing operation and for the Army troops fighting their way ashore (but they were also called upon to attack battleships). Each Taffy Group also included three destroyers and four destroyer escorts.

The Third fleet, commanded by Admiral William Halsey, included Task Force 38,commanded by Admiral Marc Mitscher, with four task groups totalling 16 "fast carriers" and Task Group 34 with 7 "fast battleships" under the command of Admiral Willis Lee. The mission of the Third Fleet was to intercept any enemy aircraft or surface units seeking to attack the Leyte Gulf landing forces. *Lexington* was assigned to Task Group 38.3. (See maneuvering chart.) This shows *Lexington* carrying Admiral Mitscher's flag. Note the four carriers in the inner ring, four battleships and four cruisers in the intermediate ring, and 18 destroyers in the outer ring. The flags of destroyer division commanders are also shown.

In addition to the names of individual ships, their radio-call names are also given. Note as well, that the *Ticonderoga* was added in a different handwriting alongside the *Princeton*, undoubtedly indicating a substitution after the *Princeton* was sunk.

For several days prior to the planned landing date at Leyte Gulf, Admiral Halsey led the Third Fleet up and down the eastern coast of the Philippine Islands in a wide sweep, attacking airfields,shipping and enemy naval units. The Third Fleet also acted as a magnet for land-based enemy aircraft, a fatal attraction that led to the destruction of hundreds of land-based aircraft.

Unfortunately, it also led to some serious damage to our own forces. On the morning of October 24th our task group was subjected to three raids by land-based planes from Luzon. Most of the 160 planes were shot down by F6Fs and AA fire but one enemy bomber came out of a cloud and

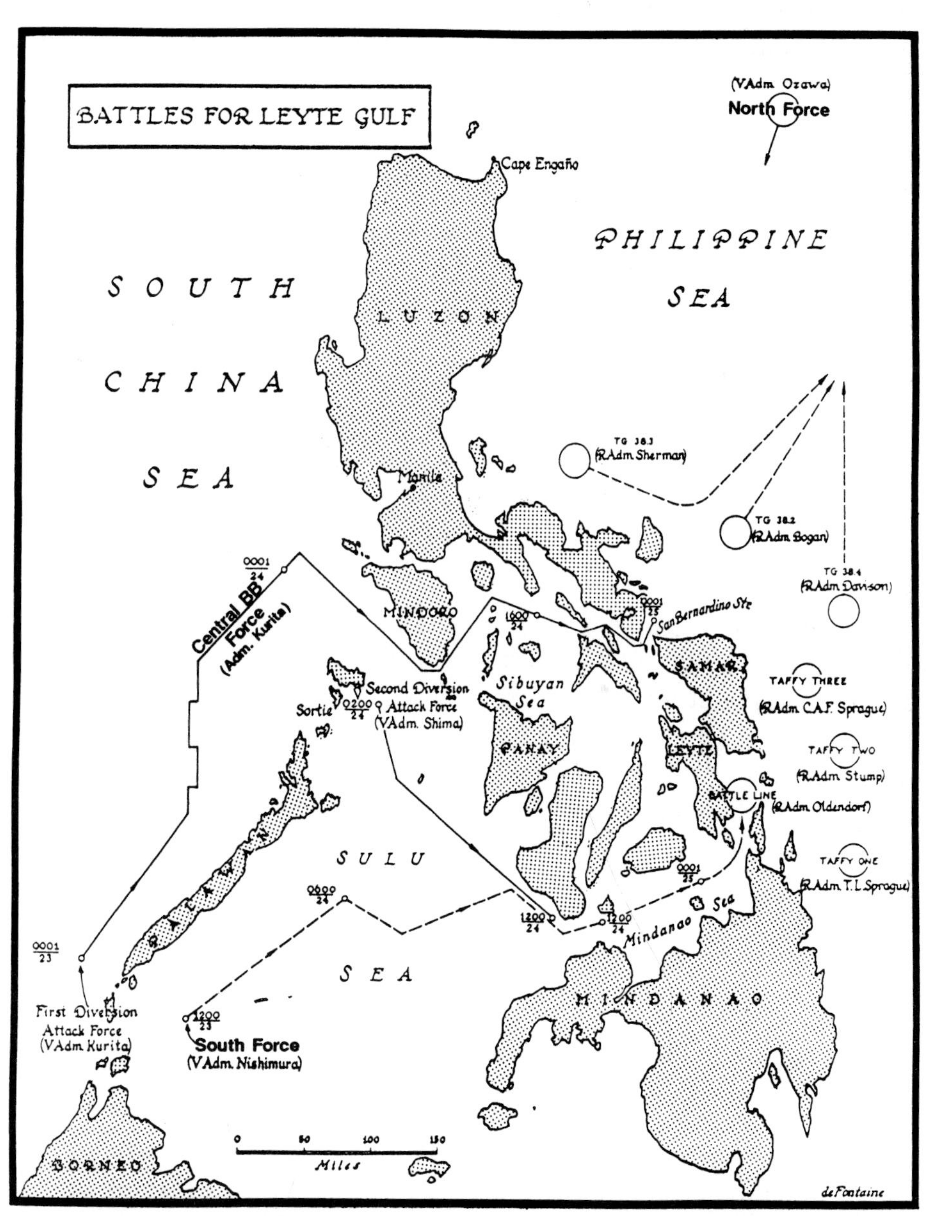

Leyte Gulf Battles – Map of U.S. and Japanese Forces.

hit USS *Princeton*, a CVL (Light Carrier) in our task group, with two bombs. At first the bomb damage seemed to be under control but delayed explosions made salvage impossible. One explosion blast struck the USS *Birmingham* which was standing by with assistance; her crew suffered more casualties than did the *Princeton*'s. Destroyers picked up survivors and distributed them among the capital ships.

The Japanese forces consisted of a southern force of two older battleships with supporting cruisers and destroyers, commanded by Admiral Nishimura, approaching Leyte Gulf through the Surigao Strait. This force was annihilated by Admiral Kincaid's Pearl Harbor battleships during the night of 24-25 October, executing a classic "crossing the Tee" maneuver, and assisted by cruisers, destroyers and PT boats. It was a sweet revenge for the "Ghost" battleships!

The Japanese had hundreds of of planes in airfields all over the Philippine Islands which were ordered to destroy the landing forces and attack U.S. forces at sea. Task Force 38 and the escort carriers in the Seventh Fleet were effective in countering these attacks.

The Japanese Northern force consisted of one first-line carrier (*Zuikaku*), three light carriers and two battleship-carriers, with supporting cruisers and destroyers, commanded by Admiral Ozawa. This group was the "bait," intended to lure Halsey's Third Fleet away from guarding the San Bernadino Strait, where the Japanese Central battleship force had to transit on their way to Leyte Gulf. The Northern force had a suicide mission and Halsey obliged them at the sacrifice of his own mission.

The Japanese Central force on 24 October consisted of five modern battleships, including two "monster" 18-inch battleships *Yamato* and *Musashi*, along with cruisers and destroyers, commanded by Admiral Kurita. This force was threading its way through the Philippine Islands headed for the San Bernadino Strait exit into the Philippine Sea; its mission was to deliver the "knock-out punch" to the Leyte Gulf landimg forces.

The Japanese Central force had been under surveillance and attack by U.S. submarines for several days. The submarines had sunk one battleship and two cruisers. As this force approached within range of Task Force 38's aircraft, a massive strike on the morning of 24 October further reduced this force, sinking *Musashi* and a cruiser. The pilots had concentrated on *Musashi* with 19 torpedo hits and a dozen bombs. The fury of the airplane attack caused Admiral Kurita to reverse course and head west. But that was only temporary.

The strike forces returned to their carriers, exuberant about their success. Their reports, along with news that Admiral Kurita was heading

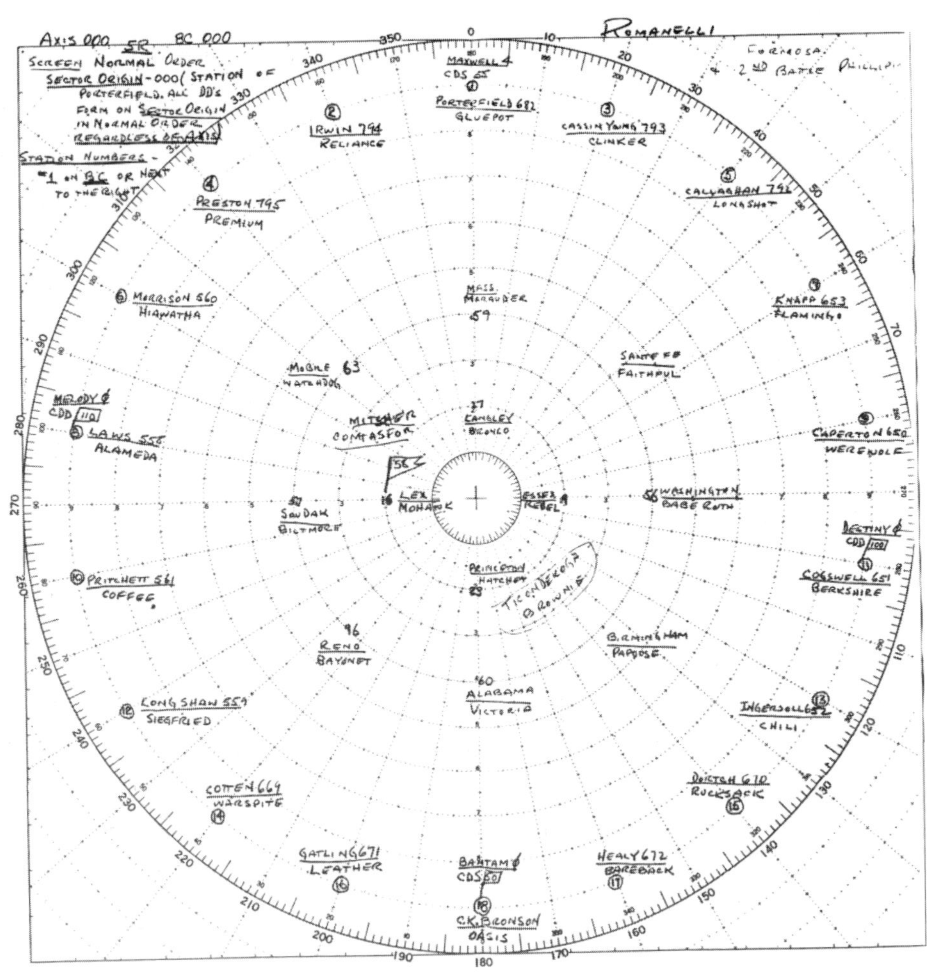

Formation of Task Group 38.3, Battle for Leyte Gulf.

west, led Halsey to believe that Kurita was retiring and abandoning his mission. That afternoon TG 38.3 was the target of a raid of more than 100 planes, from a northerly direction – the open ocean, "Ah Ha! Enemy carriers!"

The smell of enemy carriers led Admiral Halsey to indulge his obsession with the northern enemy. He ordered three task groups north (as the enemy wanted him to do). He ignored a warning from Admiral Mitscher to the effect that the battleship force was still to be accounted for. In the *Lexington* CIC we could not believe that Halsey was leaving the San Bernadino Strait unguarded!

Admiral Mitscher had two intelligence officers on his staff who had discounted the exuberance of the pilots and evaluated the situation accurately. One of these was Lt. Byron "Whizzer" White, who had attained football fame at the University of Colorado and, after the war, served 30 years as a U.S. Supreme Court Justice. But neither Lt. White nor his colleague could convince Admiral Mitscher to issue a stronger remonstrance to Admiral Halsey. What had happened was that Halsey, in his feverish impatience, had truncated the chain of command by issuing orders directly to task group commanders, bypassing Mitscher. Not kind, nor wise.

In the meantime, under cover of darkness, Admiral Kurita reversed course again and during the night exited the San Bernadino Strait and headed toward Leyte Gulf. The next morning the Taffy Three escort carriers were astounded by the 16 and 18-inch shells that were falling around them and through their thin hulls. Admiral T.L. Sprague ordered all three Taffy Groups to launch air strikes against the enemy battleships – hornets on the backs of elephants. At the same time, Admiral C.A.F. Sprague ordered his Taffy Three destroyers and destroyer escorts to attack enemy battleships. The Captains of the destroyers and destroyer escorts understood their mission quite well:

> *"Theirs not to reason why,*
> *Theirs but to do or die ...*
> *Someone had blundered"*
> (– with apologies to Alfred Lord Tennyson)

They didn't say, "How come? Why us? Where are our battleships?" They knew that they were the only surface forces available, if only they could wangle their way into close enough range to fire their torpedoes before the 18-inch and 14-inch projectiles could get them, or leap-frog between rain squalls to hide from the enemy's optical range-finders. Make smoke screens. "This is not the kind of fight we were prepared to fight; bantam weights against Joe Louis. But what the hell! Our families will be proud of our suicide mission."

"Damn the 18-imch guns. Full speed ahead!"
(– with apologies to Admiral Farragut)

Of course the outcome was inevitable. The 18-inch, 16-inch and 14-inch projectiles finally found two destroyers, one destroyer escort and two escort carriers. Five casualties of a lop-sided battle that should have been fought by Admiral Lee with his seven fast battleships. But also credit the planes from the baby flattops with a heroic defense! They sank two enemy cruisers and bombed and strafed battleships and destroyers and they so harassed Kurita that he withdrew to re-form his battle line and think about what had hit him. After thinking for three hours he decided to retreat and get back through his "rat hole" before the Third Fleet would arrive to destroy him totally.

While the three taffy groups were fighting for their lives Admiral Halsey was attacking the enemy northern force with three task groups of Task Force 38. The enemy carriers had no air defense except for their AA batteries; they had "shot their load" of aircraft the day before. In six strikes during October 25th our pilots sank all four carriers, Including *Zuikaku*, the last of the Pearl Harbor attack carriers. The two battleship-carriers got away because Halsey became distracted by a message from his boss.

While Kurita was "shooting fish in a barrel," General MacArthur sent a common language radio distress call to Admiral Nimitz. Admiral Nimitz drafted a message to Admiral Halsey, "Where is Task Force 34?" But the communications officer encoding the message followed standard practice by adding some extraneous words to baffle enemy decoders: "the whole world wonders." The complete message was transmitted to the *New Jersey*, where the decoding officer, in his rush to get the message to the admiral, forgot to strip the extraneous phrase. Nimitz' basic message would have been considered reprimand enough but Halsey was insulted by the added phrase and it infuriated him. However, he turned his three task groups around into a high-speed run south and ordered McCain's TG 38.1 to join in. But it was too late, Kurita had already escaped through the San Bernadino Strait with four battleships intact along with a few cruisers and destroyers.

That was the final action between U.S. and Japanese warships in the Leyte Gulf battle. The battle was an overwhelming victory for U.S. forces as the final score card shows; a listing of the number of ships sunk:

U.S. Forces	**Japanese**
CVL *Princeton*	CV *Zuikaku*
CVE *Gambier Bay*	CVL *Chitose*
CVE *St. Lo*	CVL *Chlyda*
2 DDs	CVL *Zuiho*
1 DE	4 BBs
1 PT	9 Cruisers
	8 DDs

U.S. losses were minor compared to total strength; our battle effectiveness was undiminished. The Japanese Navy was dead; they did not dare let their four battleships leave their home ports lest Task Force 38/58 clobber them. The only weapon left to them now was the Kamikaze which, in its defensive role, was awesome, as we would soon find out.

In the aftermath of the Leyte battle there was considerable controversy over the Halsey decision that allowed the enemy battleships to attack the baby flattops. In the 7th Fleet there was anger and anguish. In Task Force 38 there was guilt that we, with our tremendously superior force of battleships and carriers, allowed our weaker comrades-in-arms to suffer death and destruction. And why did Halsey take our battleships up north to fight carriers when their proper targets were to the south? What a disappointment! The Secretary of the Navy, James Forrestal, wanted to retire Halsey. Historian Morison charged Halsey with a "blunder." The Navy Department, in its infinite bureaucratic wisdom, rewarded Halsey with his fifth star!

Halsey was called to explain his decision to the Joint Chiefs of Staff. When asked if he would change his decision, his reply was, "Under the same circumstances, no." Some observers have asked why Halsey was not court-martialed. The answer was, "Because he was too popular."

It is interesting to examine battle strategy as followed by different commanders. Admiral Spruance was cautious, deliberate, analytical and a team player, he followed orders. The OPPLAN for the defense of the landing forces on Saipan had been prepared under the direction of Admiral Nimitz. That plan specified that the 5th Fleet "support the amphibious forces ... the covering force has the duty to engage any enemy fleet that may challenge the landing." Spruance followed this directive to the best of his judgment but certain "Hawks" criticized him for letting the surface ships escape.

Halsey did not want to be tied down by that strategy. He was a "Hawk," an impatient swashbuckler. In the OPPLAN for Leyte Gulf he insisted on the statement, "if opportunity exists or can be created, to destroy a major portion of the enemy fleet this becomes primary task." Halsey used this statement to justify his decision, his "legal" defense. He accepted no responsibility for the consequences of his actions.

In retrospect I must admit to a love-hate feeling for "Bull" Halsey. On the one hand I admire his unrelenting driving force in pursuing the enemy. He was the boldest, most active leader in the Pacific war.

American industry gave the Navy the best weapons – ships, airplanes, guns, radars – and in large quantities, The American public gave its most precious gift – its young men – intelligent, patriotic, dedicated, prepared to give their lives in the cause of freedom and the preservation of the American way of living. The cadre of competent, dedicated, professional Navy officers accepted these resources in trust and shaped them into the most powerful naval force in history. They used these resources to break the Japanese stranglehold in the Pacific.

On more than one occasion Admiral Halsey abused these resources needlessly, at the expense of ships, aircraft and many lives, all because of his egotistical pursuit of personal glory. He was reckless in leading the fleet into typhoons. His willful insistence on abandoning his primary mission in favor of targets of opportunity was intolerable and unforgivable. Finally, I take umbrage with his brusque and unkind treatment of Admiral Mitscher, a pioneer in the development of naval aviation and a leader who had respect and compassion for his subordinates.

William F. Halsey visits the Lexington 11 September 1944. (l. to r.) Vice Admiral M.A. Mitcher, Rear Admiral Carney and Admiral Halsey. (Courtesy of Robert J. Ethier)

CHAPTER 13

KAMIKAZE

After the stunning defeats in the Marianas Turkey Shoot and The Battle of Leyte Gulf, the Japanese Navy was de-fanged. They had lost most of their first-line aircraft carriers and almost all of their experienced carrier aircraft pilots. They had lost half of their most powerful battleships plus almost all of their older ones, in addition to thousands of land-based aircraft. They were running out of fuel oil and gasoline and were in desperate straits. Then they developed a weapon that suited their circumstances – the Kamikaze.

The Kamikaze ("Divine Wind") was a suicide plane. The pilot maneuvered so as to crash his plane, a bomb and himself into U.S. Navy warships. The planes did not need an aircraft carrier; they waited until our ships came within range of their land bases. They were given only enough fuel for a one-way flight. Using dive-bomber approach tactics, they were difficult to shoot down.

Psychologically, they had a devastating effect on our war-weary crews. Up until this time, our sailors could confidently count on our superior weapons, ships, aircraft and radars, which our admirals relentlessly maneuvered in pursuing the enemy; and very successfully.

How do you cope with an enemy who uses his own body as a weapon? We were not afraid to die in our mission but we had a chance to survive if we were smarter, quicker, more courageous. We would volunteer for suicide missions like the three destroyer captains who harassed the enemy battleships at Leyte Gulf; but we could survive even if our ship was sunk by 18-inch projectiles.

In a surrealistic way it almost seemed as if the only way to cope with the Japanese suicide weapon was to become suicides ourselves. Very depressing.

The escort carriers (CVEs) in the Taffy One Group during the Battle of Leyte Gulf were the targets of the first Kamikaze attacks, which caused serious damage to two escort carriers. The next target was Taffy Three, just recovering from attacks from the Japanese battleships. The CVE *St.*

Lo was sunk in this attack and there was major damage to two other CVEs. Another attack on Taffy One, by 26 Kamikazes was intercepted by our F6Fs and half of them were shot down but the remainder caused additional damage on CVEs.

The combination of the Japanese main battleship force and the Kamikaze attacks resulted in losses of three destroyers, two CVEs (*Gambier Bay* and *St. Lo*) and major damage to six other CVEs, a casualty rate of about 50%. In my book, the "baby flattops" are the true heroes of the battle of Leyte Gulf, along with the three destroyers, the Pearl Harbor battleships and the submarine force.

The successes of this first major attack by Kamikazes on our CVEs convinced the Japanese high command of the efficacy of their new weapon. In future battles, particularly as the U.S. Navy pressed closer to the Japanese homeland, the Japanese defense employed the Kamikazes with devastating effect against the U.S. Navy.

On November 3, 1944, Task Force 38 started heavy strikes against Luzon airfields and shipping in support of MacArthur's Philippine Island campaign, destroying in excess of 400 land-based aircraft.

On November 6th, four Kamikazes evaded our Combat Air Patrol (CAP). Anti-aircraft fire splashed three of them but the fourth struck the starboard side of the *Lexington's* island structure. The thud of the exploding bomb reverberated through the Combat Information Center (CIC) where I was stationed, approximately 25 feet away. The lights went out in CIC and smoke started pouring in through the ventilation system.

My roommate, Lieut. Richard Adelson, was a Communications Officer but his battle station was crew captain of a 40mm AA quad mount on the port quarter, just forward of the Landing Signal Officer's station. Normally, he would fire on targets on the port side of the ship. A firing cut-out cam prevented him from firing at low elevation targets across the flight deckk, on the starboard side. The Kamikaze was in a dive bomber approach at high elevation from the starboard side. Dick swung his gun mount across the flight deck and started firing at the rapidly approaching Kamikaze. Quite a few hits were scored which apparently killed the pilot but momentum and gravity were pulling the aircraft along its preset path to the side of *Lexington's* starboard island structure, exploding directly above the AA batteries with devastating effect on the gun crews. Dick was awarded a citation for his presence of mind in swinging his gun to bear on target.

The major casualties suffered were in the exposed areas; on the starboard side of the island, principally in the machine gun batteries; on the

Kamikaze destruction of AA batteries, starboard side, looking aft.

signal bridge all the signalmen were killed except my friend Lt. Barney Carman who received last rites from the ship's chaplain. He survived but his injuries required two years of treatment in naval hospitals before they finally healed.

A total of 50 men were killed and 132 were injured.

The Japanese pilot was wearing a parachute, for some unexplained reason, which blew upward and tangled a rotating radar antenna. Fortunately, damage to the ship's structure was superficial and did not impair battle efficiency, we continued to launch and land planes, But of course this incident provided another occasion for Tokyo Rose to sink the Blue Ghost another time. Structural repairs were made in Ulithi.

The capture of the Philippines now encouraged our Navy high command to plan for the invasion of the Japanese homeland islands. The first phase was to invade Okinawa and Iwo Jima.

We needed Iwo Jima, 800 miles from Tokyo, as a base for fighters to escort the Army B-29s bombing Japanese cities. The *Lexington* participated in the invasion of Iwo Jima; at times we steamed as close as 5 miles to the island, unusually close; while providing air support for the Marines clambering up the hillsides.

At that time, one of my roommates was the Marine major who commanded the *Lexington's* contingent of the Fleet Marine Force. With binoculars and a short-wave radio he was tuned in to the field radios of the Marines on the island who were having a rough time dislodging the entrenched Japanese defenders. He was despondent, "What am I doing here in the safety of the ship? I should be ashore, dying with my buddies."

Okinawa was needed as the air and naval base for the assault on Kyushu, the southern-most Japanese home island. In preparation for this assault, the Fifth Fleet, now commanded by Admiral Spruance, steamed up and down the eastern coast of the home islands attacking airfields and military and industrial targets.

Admiral Halsey has been quoted as saying that he was scared by the effectiveness of the Kamikaze attacks. He was reflecting a fleet-wide feeling. But he was not cringing. He devised changes in tactics and exhorted his subordinates to strengthen their resolve and give no quarter to the enemy.

Among the changes devised on the *Lexington* to cope with the Kamikaze threat, was one that involved my roommate Lt. Richard Morland. Morland's usual GQ station was in CIC, as assistant Fighter-Director. To cope with low-flying enemy aircraft that eluded radar detection beyond the horizon, Morland was stationed on a visual observation platform at

USS Franklin – here pictured dead in the water only 50 miles off the coast of Formosa. Revived and sheltered out of the war zone, she made it back under her own power to the Brooklyn Navy Yard for repair, but never made it back to active service.

the top of the island structure, 150 feet above sea level. There, with a pair of binoculars and in direct radio communication with the Combat Air Patrol, he scanned the horizon and could immediately vector the CAP to intercept.

Like my regard for Winston Churchill, I considered this time to be Halsey's "finest hour." His words provided some balm to the weary hearts of officers and men throughout the fleet. I was glad to see a compassionate spark of humanity in the old salt's character.

To cope with the Kamikaze threat, the fleet withdrew to Ulithi for a brief rest and to develop some new defensive tactics against the Kamikazes. One such tactic involved stationing a line of destroyers as picket ships between the enemy airfields and the carriers. We also doubled the number of fighter squadrons, night and day, to create a "blanket" of Combat Air Patrol over the enemy airfields.

The *Lexington* was fortunate to be reprieved from the coming fury of the Okinawa campaign. In the battle plans for Task Group 58.2, distributed in Ulithi in March of 1945, the *Lexington* was listed to participate in the next action against Okinawa. But two days before sortie time, a new Essex-class carrier, the *USS Franklin*, arrived at Ulithi Atoll and was assigned our role in the Okinawa campaign, lock, stock and barrel.

In its first engagement, the *Franklin*, unfortunately, was the target of enemy bombs which left it crippled and dead in the water, just 50 miles from the nearest Japanese mainland. But it did not sink; it found its way back to the Brooklyn Navy Yard under its own power.

The *Lexington* was relieved of its assignment in the Fast Carrier Task Force and returned to our home port of Bremerton, Washington. We had been on the cutting edge of the action for 13 months, longer than any other "fast carrier" in the Pacific. The ship was in need of overhaul and the crew was in need of R & R.

One of my roommates, Lt. Richard Adelson was a communications officer. His job aboard the *Lexington* had been to operate the super-secret machines that encoded and decoded secret radio messages.

When plans were made to operate in conjunction with the British Navy, Dick was assigned to a British command ship in Australian waters as liaison officer to handle all secret radio messages between U.S. Navy and British Navy forces.

After 2 $^1/_2$ years on the *Lexington* I was assigned to the Gunnery Officers Ordnance School in Washington, D.C. where I served as an instructor in Fire Control Systems until February 1946, when I was released to inactive duty.

But our hearts and minds were still with the fleet supporting the invasion of Okinawa. The Japanese defense, using the Kamikazes, was the most furious of all the campaigns during the war. The destroyers in the picket line now became prime targets for the Kamikazes; several were sunk.

The "fast carriers" took a beating. The *Franklin* and *Intrepid* had to be withdrawn because of serious damage. They suffered from the common vulnerability of having wooden decks. They've been characterized as "Joe Louis with a glass jaw." A bomb hit on the flight deck could be devastating. This was in contrast to the British carriers, which had steel armor plated decks which prevented penetration.

In the Okinawa campaign, the British Navy sent a complete task force, including several aircraft carriers to assist our Fast Carrier Task Force.

The Japanese battleship *Yamato*, the world's largest, with 18-inch gun barrels had been holed up in a homeland port since the Battle of Leyte Gulf. The Japanese high command did not want to risk having it being sunk by the Fast Carrier Task Force. But when the action for the defense of Okinawa became desperate, the Emperor was petitioned to permit the *Yamato* to bring about its own glorious demise alongside the Kamikaze airplanes.

A U.S. submarine report advised Admiral Mitscher when the *Yamato* left port and Task Force 58 was immediately dispatched to engage it. Strikes of more than 500 sorties put a dozen bombs and 10 torpedoes into the monster and she sank in the imperial watery graveyard amidst thousands of Kamikaze buddies. A final example of the dominance of the airplane over the battleship.

The furious defenses of Iwo Jima and Okinawa were fearsome harbingers of what awaited our forces when we invaded the Japanese homeland. And thus, there was a great sigh of relief when the atomic bombing of Hiroshima and Nagasaki convinced the Japanese to surrender. It was estimated that "The Bomb" saved the lives of one million American soldiers, airmen and sailors and probably ten times that many Japanese military and civilian lives.

I say, "Thank God for The Bomb." I have no respect for the handwringing liberals who accuse our armed forces, our President and the majority of the American people for the deaths of the inhabitants of Hiroshima and Nagasaki. War is hell but it's worse if you don't win it.

And so we close the circle to the pacifists in Union Square in the 1930s.

CHAPTER 14
POST WAR

I was relieved of active duty on "points" (length of service) on a Friday in February 1946. After a weekend of partying with friends and family, I wasted no time looking for a job. Two days later I landed an engineering job with the Consolidated Edison Waterside power plant in New York City. I was anxious to get started in my civilian career. After three years and eight months of Navy wartime service, I was weary of battles, destruction and the loss of young lives. I felt I had paid my dues to liberty and country.

My two stateroom 103 roommates were also released from active duty and pursued civilian careers. Richard Adelson joined the management of his family's confectionary plant but later switched to his first love and became an antique book dealer, working out of Vermont.

Richard Morland resumed his academic career to earn a Ph.D. in philosophy, followed by a professorship at a Florida University.

For four years, I settled down to civilian living, married and started a family. But I was still a Naval Reserve officer, though on inactive status. In 1950 the Navy Department offered reserve officers a two-week course on guided missiles at John Hopkins University. I was intrigued at the chance to learn about the latest advance in fire control technology, so I applied for the course.

Recognizing my continued interest in Naval fire control advances, in 1951 the Navy Department decided to promote me to the permanent rank of Lieutenant Commander. In addition, in a correspondence course, my solution to a fleet movement logistics and fueling problem was well received at the Naval War College. But in 1962 I was officially retired, much to my wife Dorothy's relief.

Later I started attending reunions of former *Lexington* crew members and reviving 45-year-old memories meeting my former roommates, Dick Adelson and Dick Morland, and some of my 8th Division crew. On two occasions I was moved to write poems to express my feelings. These poems were read at the formal dinners at the reunions and evoked expres-

To the Crew of '89 From the Crew of '44

(Written the week after the plane crash that caused five fatalities)

Two generations span our years
But we are here to share your tears
It was the same season in forty-four
That the Kamikaze hit during the war.
Your late shipmates now join the ranks
Of other brave soldiers to whom our nation
owes much thanks.
Let the blood that has stained these decks
Accrue to the honor of our Lady Lex.
So let us mourn but also be proud
And carry on with heads unbowed.
May your grief be brief and your memory long,
May your hearts be tender and your spirits strong.

– Otto Romanelli

Brotherhood

(Prepared for USS Lexington Reunion, Lexington, KY 19 September 1998)

Those that go down to the sea in ships
Share the dangers of Nature's fury
And the bombs and torpedoes of enemy fire.
These risks form bonds stronger than those of blood
And create the extended family of brotherhood
Our youthful abandon spurred commitment to
flag and nation,
Unconcerned of danger to life and limb.
Those of our brothers who paid the ultimate price
Have earned our devotion to their memory
And cemented the bonds of our surviving brotherhood.
I salute you brothers, one and all.

– Otto Romanelli

sions of reciprocal feelings from former shipmates. They were printed in the *Lexington* Association's "Sunrise Press."

I was greeted at one reunion by Bob Letts, a fire controlman who, during the war was barely 18 years old and still growing. At that time I was 5 feet 10 inches tall. At the reunion in 1989 he heard that I was present and he instructed his wife to look for a tall guy. We finally met. Over the years, I had shrunk to 5 feet 8 inches and he had grown to 6 feet. He no longer had to look up to me.

At another reunion I was greeted by "Smokey" Gerhard, a gunner's mate. He put his hand in his pocket and pulled out a nondescript token.

"Do you remember when you gave me this?" (This was 46 years earlier).

"No, I can't say that I do."

"Well, you gave me this when you made me the division's leading petty officer. It allowed me to go to the head of the chow line. But later you threatened to put me on report."

"What for?"

"For fighting with the First Lieutenant's clerk, who wouldn't give me deck paint even though I had a signed requisition. Our spaces were bare and rusting and you had told me to get them painted or we would get an 'unsatisfactory' at inspection time."

"So what happened? Did I send you up to Captain's Mast?"

"No. You said I had adequate justification to nail him."

After the war, like my own release from active duty, the *Lexington* was briefly decommissioned. But after the Korean War she was reactivated and modernized with an angled deck and enclosed forecastle (see photo). Assigned to the Seventh Fleet, she did guard duty in the Far East and Cuba.

In 1962 the *Lexington* was assigned to Pensacola, Florida as a training ship for new pilots. She accumulated a lifetime record, probably never to be surpassed, of landings and take-offs in excess of 500,000. She was finally de-commissioned in 1991 and is now berthed in Corpus Christi, Texas as part of the Museum on the Bay. In her final retirement, the "Blue Ghost" serves a new role, as a living legend.

INDEX

NOTES

The "Blue Ghost" circa 1962, with enclosed fo'c's'le and angled deck.